Red Pepper

". . . the red hair and now poetry. Poetry! He gets more like F.C. every day." Simon has always been the odd one out in the Pepper family, but when he overhears his mother's comment he begins to wonder if he belongs to them at all!

Determined to discover the link between himself and the mysterious F.C., and to establish his real identity, Simon asks his friend Morgan to help him. The boys try to piece together the Pepper family tree – Simon's grandparents are delighted to dig out faded photographs and to talk endlessly about old times, though his mother becomes quite concerned by his new obsession with his blood! They travel to London to look at birth and marriage certificates, and then the final clue arrives. The dramatic events which follow show Simon where he really belongs!

Red Pepper is Pauline Hunt's first novel. She is an experienced writer and journalist, and now works on the *Cambridge Evening News*.

Red Pepper

Pauline Hunt

Hippo Books
Scholastic Publications Ltd
London

Scholastic Publications Ltd,
141–143 Drury Lane, London, WC2B 5TG,
England
Scholastic Book Services,
50 West 44th Street, New York, NY 10036, USA
Scholastic Tab Publications Ltd,
123 Newkirk Road, Richmond Hill,
Ontario L4C 3G5 Canada
Ashton/Scholastic, Box 579,
Gosford, New South Wales, Australia
Ashton/Scholastic,
9–11 Fairfax Avenue, Penrose, Auckland,
New Zealand

First published by Scholastic Publications Ltd 1983

Made and printed in Great Britain by
Cox & Wyman Ltd,
Reading
Phototypeset in Plantin Roman by
Input Typesetting Ltd,
London SW19 8DR

CHAPTER ONE

"Simon has ability but will not apply himself to his work."
"Simon lacks self-discipline. He must learn to work at things which do not immediately attract him."
"Simon is too easily satisfied with less than his best."
"If Simon day-dreamed less and worked more he would do well."

A chorus of different voices chased each other round and round in Simon's head, echoing the comments that appeared on his end of term report. He trudged up the long road of neat, identical semi-detached houses, weighed down with a half-open satchel, a grubby school bag full of sports equipment, and the brown envelope containing his report sticking out of his blazer pocket.

He hoisted his satchel a little higher on his shoulder – its weight had pulled his blazer quite out of shape – as he turned into the garden of number 52, feeling the tired, dusty figure that he looked, his shoe laces trailing along after him. He wasn't looking forward to the reception his report was going to get. Perhaps he should save the only good news till later.

Mrs Pepper was on her knees weeding the back garden when she heard the sound of Simon opening the door. She came in immediately, arriving just as he dropped everything in the middle of the spotless kitchen floor. Automatically she picked up the shoes he had kicked off.

"I'll make you a cup of tea." She turned round from washing her hands and noticed the brown report envelope on the kitchen table. Simon's sharp glance saw the flicker cross her face, the tightening of the muscles.

"Is it any better?" she asked, trying hard to disguise the slightly anxious, querulous tone.

"Not much," he answered truthfully. "I did try at the. . . " He broke off. His mother had stopped listening. She was reading.

She put down the report and went over to the sink to fill the kettle.

"You've got a very good mark for English," she commented in flat, measured tones.

Simon nodded.

"I like old Marchington. He's really good. He asked to see me this morning to give me a pep talk about trying harder at the things I didn't like." Simon paused to make sure she was listening. "Then he said they had decided to give me a prize."

"Simon, how absolutely marvellous. I always knew you were really bright," his mother exclaimed excitedly.

She rushed up to him and rumpled his thick, red, curly hair. Simon's self-consciousness was tinged with guilt and resentment. It was no good pretending. He had never tried much at school. If only his parents would not pin so much hope on him. . .

Debbie clattered into the room, and grabbed a biscuit before picking up Simon's report and attempting to decipher the sprawling, illegible writing.

"Debbie's report is lying around somewhere," said Mrs Pepper. "She has got an A for art."

"Good," said Simon with as much enthusiasm as he could muster. If only Debbie were cleverer she could have taken her share of the awful burden of their parents' hopes and dreams.

"My report is just as good as Simon's," Debbie pointed out defensively.

"Simon has got a school prize," his mother announced with evident joy.

"What for?"

"English."

"No, actually it is for poetry," Simon corrected her.

"Poetry!" Disbelief and pain registered in his mother's high-pitched exclamation. "Not poetry, Simon?"

A wave of anger swept through Simon's entire body. "What is wrong with writing poetry?" he shouted. The edgy, metallic tone of his voice was something over which he had no control. Even as he spoke he knew at the back of his mind that, of course, his parents would not like poetry. Why else did he carefully hide his poems away when everything else was left carelessly lying around?

His mother was visibly shivering despite the warm afternoon, and put her hands round her teacup for comfort. She struggled to regain her composure.

"I don't expect Shakespeare's parents felt ashamed of him." Even in the high fever of temper Simon felt ashamed of the childishness of his sarcasm. He knew he must get out.

Debbie, alarmed and uncomprehending, was trying to comfort her mother.

"We write lots and lots of poems at school. Boys as well as girls."

Simon deliberately crashed the kitchen door behind him as he sought shelter in his own room. His anger was desperately searching for an outlet. He glanced round the room looking for something to break.

His eyes swept the shelves, the ornaments, the globe, the desk, the dictionary and atlas. . . all things required to turn him into the tidy, hard-working son his parents longed for. He couldn't bring himself to destroy anything. They had put so much love and care into it all. But nothing, just *nothing* of it was him. He couldn't even leave his papers lying around without his mother clearing them away. It was all for the son they hoped he would be. Unable to bear his rage any longer he grabbed a book, shoved it into his pocket and charged out of the house.

"Simon!" He ignored his mother's call as he vanished down the road. He hadn't consciously thought where he was going, but instinctively headed for the nearest patch of wild land. It wasn't a particularly lovely spot. Arguments raged constantly over whether it was to become a housing estate or remain an open space. But meanwhile it was simply neglected, and a jumbly thicket had begun to take possession. It was the place Simon went when he was unhappy. There was one spot under the bushes that he had made into his own den. There he could sit quietly, cut off from the rest of the world, just thinking and being himself.

A great deal of time seemed to have passed when, tired and uncomfortable, he sloped back home. He was stepping over the rubble left by the builders who were working on the extension to the house when he heard his parents' voices floating out of open French windows.

". . . the red hair and now poetry. Poetry! He gets more like F.C. every day."

Simon stood quite still, startled by the words he heard and only half comprehending his father's reply.

"That is not the point, Chrissie. Those are only the superficialities. Simon is quite a different person underneath."

Simon was struggling to make sense of the name his mother had spoken. He hadn't quite caught it. Was it F. Seed, Effie, F.C.? Whatever it was he had never heard it before. Not only that, it was the first time in his life anybody had ever said he was like someone else. The family always insisted he was one on his own.

He longed to hear more. But his basic honesty made him step heavily on the crunchy gravel to warn his parents of his arrival.

They both looked up self-consciously. Clearly

anxious to forget the earlier scene his mother hurried out to fetch the supper she had kept hot for him.

Mr Pepper was sitting back comfortably in an easy chair, the evening paper over his knee. Simon looked at him and experienced, as he had many times before, a great sense of distance between himself and his father. Physically they could not be less alike. His father was broad-shouldered and strongly built. With his closely-cut hair and conventional clothes he looked exactly the responsible, utterly reliable local government officer that he was. Good-natured and popular, his bearing radiated the self confidence of his commonsense "I know what I like" philosophy.

His wife came back into the living room.

"Debbie has a nasty graze on her foot from her roller skates," she said anxiously. "Would you go up and look at it, Cyril? Perhaps I should take her to the doctor's tomorrow to get it dressed?"

"It won't be anything much." Flat and unsympathetic though the response sounded Mr Pepper dutifully went upstairs to examine the foot.

Simon wondered if his mother ever stopped worrying about something. She picked up the *Daily Express* and looked through it fitfully, every now and then twisting her hair round one of her fingers. As soon as he could, Simon escaped to the privacy of his own bedroom. He wanted to read but his mind had the exhausted waywardness that follows anger and makes concentration impossible. Time and time again it insisted on replaying the events of the last few hours.

He stared at his reflection in the mirror. Skinny with clear blue eyes, his bony features were covered with the freckles that so often go with ginger hair. The red hair, the brilliance of which was unmatched in his school, had earned him the nickname "Red" Pepper.

Who was it in the family who looked like this? If there was anybody who had red hair he had never discovered him. Now for the very first time he was convinced he had a kinsman. Red hair and poetry? Simon already felt close to him. But what possible reason could his parents have to hide the truth? What had this man done to make them so ashamed of him?

Gradually an idea began to take shape. Whoever it might be, somehow or other he was going to track down this relative. He did not know where to start but it shouldn't be too hard finding one's family. He would have time. It was the start of the summer holidays. Excitement soared within him.

It would be a detective exercise to find the missing link. He resolved to start by trying to work out a family tree. He grabbed a piece of paper and a biro and began to sketch in the names of the relatives he knew.

There was his father Cyril Pepper. His sister, Aunt Beryl, now Mrs Allen, and her children, David, Susan and Jane. No Effie or F.C. there.

Next came grandfather Frank Pepper. He could possibly be called Frank Cyril (F.C.?). But that didn't seem a very promising idea. Grandfather Pepper had been a sports-mad, chatty greengrocer – no red-haired poet by any stretch of the imagination.

Grandma was called Lily. Simon cast around for clues to her maiden name. He fed the problem into the computer in his brain. The process often worked. Give it a little time to play over the questions and it would punch out the answer. Rigby. That was it. The name they put on the label of the calendar they always sent to her brother in Canada. It was quite possible there were some red-haired relatives there, but since none of them had ever come back to this country, it was hard to see why anybody should be worried about them.

Simon switched his attention to his mother's side of the family. Chrissie as she was always called. He wrote carefully against Cyril's name "married Christine Woodbyrne". His grandparents on her side he knew as Jenny and Pop; something that had always surprised him – they had never seemed that sort of modern-minded family.

His mother was an only child. Or. . .the idea began to take root, supposing she wasn't? Could there be a black-sheep brother they were all ashamed of? Simon crossed out Pop and substituted his proper name Edgar. He simply could not recollect Jenny's maiden name. All he did remember was her description of the very strict father who had brought her up on his own after the early death of her mother; he couldn't recall ever hearing of any brothers and sisters.

Already the family tree had developed into a sprawling, untidy tangle. There were a lot of gaps he was going to have to fill in. Pop's widowed sister, for instance. He had a lot of work ahead.

Simon could hear his parents talking long after he climbed into bed. The clear summer evening light streamed into his room, and he pulled the bedcovers over his head to escape into the comforting, velvety darkness. But his mind refused to relax. Ideas chased each other round like dodgem cars, occasionally colliding. Suddenly several ideas crashed into one another with a blinding flash of light.

Of course, that was the answer. That was why they didn't approve of F.C. Why they didn't want to know about him. Everything fell into place. F.C. didn't fit into the family tree at all. Not the Peppers' family tree at least.

Simon was adopted! With a marvellous sense of liberation he realized he didn't belong to the Peppers, or Chaucer Road, at all. F.C., whoever he was, must be his real father. That was why he was different. Why hadn't he thought of it before? He felt a great wave of optimism and elation sweep over him. Somewhere there was a person – and a place – to whom he truly belonged. He was determined to find them.

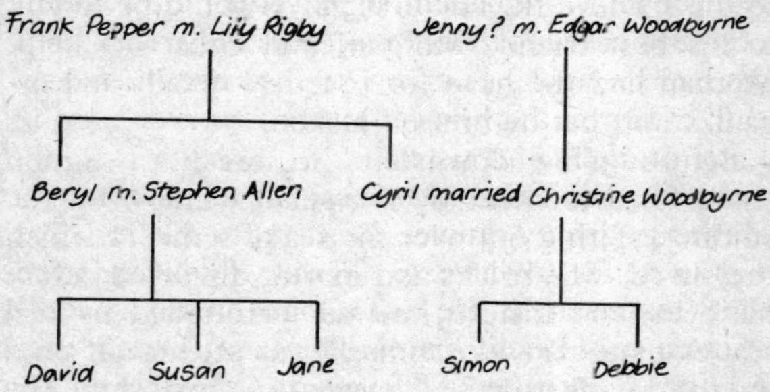

CHAPTER TWO

When he woke up Simon's sense of urgency was mixed with frustration at the enormous task ahead of him. Where was he to start? He knew himself all too well. He was a dreamer: very good on plans and ambitions, but very poor when it came down to the spadework. His first move would be to talk to his best friend, Morgan, and enlist his help. Morgan had the head for practical details and organization that he himself lacked.

Before going downstairs to breakfast Simon stood for a moment by the small window on the landing, staring out over the sea of semis in which they lived. The bricks and mortar dissolved before his eyes, and instead he was surrounded by real sea. A man very like himself was setting off on a long and dangerous sea voyage in a small ship. His young wife was standing on the quayside waving goodbye, holding their small son in her arms.

Simon's imagination sped over the weeks of the voyage, the sailor sitting in his tiny cabin writing his diary, every now and then adding a few verses to his epic poem. On and on until the tragic, fatal moment when the little ship was dashed against the rocks in a furious storm at sea.

Back home the delicate wife, now ailing and distraught when every day failed to bring news of her husband, gave way to despair. She grew slowly weaker and weaker. . . till the sad day when the baby boy was left an orphan, without a relative in the world. Eventually a kindly couple, not far removed in his imagination from the Peppers, came forward and offered to care for the child bringing him up as their own son. He began to embellish the saga with details – the truly great poem was retrieved much later in a waterproof case . . . Suddenly his mother's voice interrupted his thoughts.

Mrs Pepper was relieved to find Simon in such good spirits and warmly approved of his plan to go and see Morgan. She always lived in hope that some of his friend's studious and painstaking habits would rub off on him.

Simon swallowed his tea and toast in an atmosphere filled with the smell of warm, soapy water. Mrs Pepper was feeding his sports wear into the washing machine.

"There's mould on these shorts," she exclaimed. "You must have screwed them up when they were still. . . "

"Sorry about that. I'd better be off now."

"Simon you will tidy your bedroom before. . . "

He was out of the door before she had finished the sentence.

"Take care on your bike," she called after him.

Morgan's house was situated near the town centre in the old part of town. It was a hotchpotch of rows of small, old terraced houses opening straight on to the pavement, corner shops and warehouses, and a few roads of gaunt, tall Victorian houses.

It was in one of these Victorian houses that the Thomases lived. They lived near the centre of town because they didn't own a car. Neither, for that matter, did they have a television set or telephone. On principle. Mr Pepper labelled them uncharitably the "brown rice and duffle coat brigade".

Simon propped his bike against the dilapidated fence. The metal bell-pull delivered a clanging noise which resounded throughout the house and brought a temporary halt to the gratings and squeakings of one small Thomas practising on the violin.

Mrs Thomas threw open the door in her warm, extravagant way. She was dramatically dressed in a full-length Indian garment and open-toed sandals. Simon walked past the burgundy paintwork which someone had abruptly finished halfway down the hallway.

"It is marvellous about your poetry prize, Pep. Absolutely super."

"Yes, but it is not officially announced yet."

"Don't worry, I shan't tell a soul."

Morgan was sprawled over one side of the large breakfast table struggling with the *Guardian* crossword. Simon's entrance gave him a much welcome opportunity to abandon it without losing face in front of his younger brothers.

In the midst of the pots of marmalade and packets of cereal Evan was busily assembling an aeroplane, calling into operation spare teaspoon handles whenever they came in useful. Llewellyn rushed in spilling a handful of earth over the matting clutching a centipede, and at just the same moment the violinist made his appearance.

"You were playing really well this morning."

Madoc greeted his mother's encouragement with a mixture of disbelief and gratitude. Meanwhile she guided the smallest Thomas back into the garden gently explaining how a centipede got its name.

This was Simon's idea of what family life ought to be! Morgan, who experienced its delights at much closer quarters, was much more conscious of its drawbacks. He had spent twenty minutes trying unsuccessfully to track down a clean pair of socks without holes.

Mrs Thomas was a Londoner. When she fell in love with Mr Thomas she had embraced, in her romantic fervour, all things Welsh. Hence the music, or more accurately the repetitious chords and discords, punctuated by angry pauses, as small boys struggled with a variety of difficult instruments.

Welsh poems, Welsh holidays in the mountains. . . what Mr Thomas felt about it all was unrecorded. He seemed to glide through the house at intervals, and occasionally the sound of a typewriter floated down from one of the upstairs rooms.

Mrs Thomas was gathering up a few dishes as Morgan and Simon rose to leave. "Going anywhere interesting?"

"No." Morgan adjusted the steel-rimmed, thick-lensed glasses, which gave him an owlish, intellectual look. He never said more than was strictly necessary and rarely smiled.

Simon left his bike attached to the railings. Morgan disliked cycling – largely because he so often fell off his bike. He was an ungainly boy with arms and legs that looked too long for his body. He was easily the clumsiest boy in Simon's class.

As they ambled towards the river, Simon wondered how best to broach the subject of his parentage. Finally he simply blurted out, "I think I'm adopted."

Morgan turned to study him, raising his eyebrows slightly. Simon related yesterday's events.

"Not much evidence," said Morgan.

"Well, what about my appearance? My hair and my face. Anyone can see your family are all related; you're all alike."

Morgan didn't like that very much. "I don't know about that. I've heard of people getting red hair from their grandparents. It quite often skips a generation."

"My grandparents haven't got red hair. I know them all."

"Perhaps it can skip two generations. I'll ask Mum. She'll be absolutely delighted. She is always terribly keen to discuss these things with us." Morgan paused.

"There is another possibility," he said thoughtfully. "You can find out from your blood group. I read that if you had a different blood group from your parents then they could not actually be your parents, if you see what I mean."

Morgan's logical, precise mind seemed to endear him more to the masters at school than Simon's undisciplined imagination. Nevertheless theorising about blood groups was one thing; establishing proof quite another.

Apart from such crazy schemes as waving the

bread knife carelessly around the meal table, or taking a syringe into the Peppers' bedroom at night, Simon could imagine no way of obtaining the necessary samples, let alone getting them analysed.

"You could start by asking them," suggested Morgan prosaically. "You parents probably have cards stating their category. I got one when I had my tonsils out. I am group O." The information was delivered in such a way it sounded like a status symbol.

They were sitting by the river, staring vacantly at the water when Morgan scotched the whole theory.

"You can't be adopted. Not unless you think Debbie is as well."

Simon had to think about that for a few moments.

"No, she isn't. She looks like Dad. And the other day the relatives were all nattering about whether she was a real Pepper or not."

"And what did they say about you."

"They didn't. They never do. That's the point. The whole thing is a mystery."

"Well why should your parents adopt you when they were able to have their own children? I shouldn't think it was because you were such a beautiful baby!"

There was a hint of a smile on Morgan's face but Simon chose to ignore the remark. "Well, they could have taken me in, out of the goodness of their hearts. Perhaps I was abandoned."

"You were probably left on the Town Hall steps by a poor, starving young woman one cold Christmas Day." Morgan laughed, remembering where

Mr Pepper worked. "But I don't think things like that happen any more. If they did they would be across all the papers. *Somebody* would have told you."

Simon outlined the story he had dreamed up at the landing window, toning it down a bit because of Morgan's keen sense of the ridiculous.

Morgan's silence was more telling than comment.

"You could," he suggested with apparent seriousness, "be the direct descendant of the last of the Tsars, smuggled out of Russia and carried in a blanket to Chaucer Road. Didn't Catherine the Great have red hair?"

That really was too much, even for Simon.

"All right, forget it. I'm off. Just don't repeat what I've told you to anyone. I'll find out by myself." Simon rose to go. Privately he rather liked the Romanoff idea but even he had to acknowledge it was pushing it a bit far.

"Keep your hair on and sit down," said Morgan. "You have to analyse things sensibly and I'm not convinced about the adoption theory. I'm sure your parents would have told you. After all it is nothing to be ashamed about, and they are just the sort of people who would want to do things the correct way." Simon could see Morgan's point.

"But there is a mystery," his friend continued. "The most likely possibility is that this man F.C. is a relative who has done something awful. Perhaps he's in jail!"

That didn't appeal at all. Already in Simon's eyes F.C. was a romantic hero. He searched fruitlessly through his pockets for his scribbled family tree. Blast! He must have left it on the pillow. He hastily outlined the general pattern of his father's family.

"Your father could have had a brother." That suggestion struck a chord in Simon's mind. He closed his eyes searching for clues. It was like trying to find a card in a library filing system when you could remember neither the author nor the book title.

Suddenly a picture flashed before his eyes. A photograph of his father, quite small, sitting on Grandma's knee with Grandad holding Aunt Beryl and, he was sure, a taller boy standing on one side.

"Right," announced Morgan, flushed with the success of his first suggestion. "This afternoon we'll pay a courtesy call on your grandparents."

Courtesy calls didn't come naturally to Simon, but lunchtime provided him with just the excuse he needed. A letter had come from Jenny and Pop accepting an invitation to stay at Chaucer Road. That in itself would be a help in Simon's quest.

But the more immediate problem was that Grandma Pepper's iron had broken. She needed one urgently and the Peppers had a spare. Simon's mother was caught up in a succession of chores, messages for elderly neighbours and some promised flower arranging for a friend's anniversary, so she was relieved and delighted by Simon's unexpected offer to help.

Nevertheless she had to call Simon back as he set off once more for Morgan's house, minus the iron. "Don't leave it on the bus whatever you do." Since Simon had started at the high school she had become very familiar with the bus company's lost property office.

Seated on the top of the double decker Simon

explained to Morgan how everything was falling neatly into place.

"It will be spring cleaning yet again in our house because Jenny and Pop – that's Mum's parents – are coming to stay."

"Did you inquire about blood groups?"

"Oh, no! That went right out of my head."

"Well I asked about red hair. Mum got out the encyclopaedia. Apparently a man called Mendel crossed tall pea plants with short pea plants. The next lot of pea plants they produced were all tall. But when they were crossed again some were tall and some were short. They were the grandchildren so to speak. What it all means is that parents can pass on to their children characteristics that seem to have been lost for a generation or two."

Simon looked rather unimpressed at the end of this narrative so Morgan took out a notebook and drew a rough plan of the pea family, complete with tall and short members, to explain it more clearly.

"I get it." Simon felt slightly insulted at being compared to a pea. The last of the Tsars was much more romantic. He was decidedly reluctant to write off the adoption theory. It had all sorts of possibilities.

Meanwhile Morgan was doggedly pursuing the mundane realities.

"Does your grandfather have grey hair?"

"Yes."

"Do you remember what colour it was before?"

"No, but it can't have been red or my mother would have told me when I asked."

"Well we'll have to ask. That is the first thing to discover."

Simon agreed without enthusiasm. He found it

difficult enough to carry on a conversation with his grandparents without asking if they had had a son who died or disappeared. Not to mention finding out what colour Grandad's hair used to be!

It was Morgan who remembered to pick up the iron from where they had put it, at their feet, on the floor of the bus.

CHAPTER THREE

Grandma looked surprised when Simon, uncharacteristically, accepted her offer to stay and have a cup of tea. She led the boys into a sitting room where Grandad's huge frame was wedged into a large armchair. Nowadays he walked only with difficulty and had become quite deaf.

He tried to rise but Grandma stopped him. "Don't get up Frank. The boys understand."

A huge Alsatian stretched out at his feet, giving the whole room a doggy smell which mingled with the scent of Grandad's tobacco. The boys edged their way between a quantity of large, heavy furniture. There was barely room to move.

There were ornaments everywhere, on the television, the mantelpiece, the piano, the sideboard, in and out of the display cabinet. There were even brass ornaments in the fireplace where a large coal fire glowed despite the bright sunshine outside. The heat and atmosphere were oppressive.

"How are you getting on at school then?" Grandad inquired genially.

"Not very well." Simon mouthed his reply.

"I expect you would rather be out on a field having a good game of football, eh?" Grandad gave them both a huge wink.

Simon simply smiled back. He had learned not to draw attention to the fact that he didn't like football, and that the games afternoon at school was absolute torture. It wasn't that he didn't try, but his inclusion in any team was a penalty in itself.

He had learned the hard way that boys must like football as well as pop music. Just as it spelt disaster to admit to enjoying poetry, let alone writing it. He still smarted from the indignity of being branded Percy Bysshe Pepper by one of the form bullies.

Grandma manoeuvred her way through the furniture to deposit a heavy tray of tea things. Simon leaped up to help her.

"Come on then woman. Don't be slow about it." The Peppers senior always addressed each other in a growly banter.

"You are getting no chocolate cake with your waistline," she retorted.

"She never has fed me properly you know. Have to do everything for myself." He gave a large wink.

"You'd be a fine one. . . "

"Who is that in the photograph?" Simon interrupted, pointing to a picture on a cabinet. He hated this sort of repartee even if it was well-intentioned.

"Grandad's sister, Joyce." Grandma reached over for the picture and gave it to Simon at the same time as offering him a piece of chocolate cake. He was already balancing a cup of tea on his knee.

He had gingerly rested the cup and the photo on

the arm of his chair just as Morgan leapt up awkwardly to take a cup from Grandma. Simon grabbed his cup as a tidal wave swept across the settee, and the picture went crashing to the floor accompanied by the sound of breaking glass.

He was flushed and embarrassed. "I'm terribly sorry," he stuttered.

Deftly Grandma seized the ornamental brush and dustpan from the hearth and swept up the bits of glass. "Not to worry. I have already smashed a plate today. I must remember to break a match. Things always happen in threes," she added portentously.

While she was searching for a matchstick Simon bent down to pick up the photograph. Several others had been tucked away behind it.

His eye was caught by an old sepia studio portrait of a handsome, moustached young man, wearing a flashy pin-stripe suit and sporting a carnation buttonhole. The toothy smile radiated self-satisfaction.

This was a new face. Certainly it wasn't anybody Simon had ever seen. "Who is this?" he asked.

Grandma's hand stretched out to take back the picture. "Just an old friend of the family," she said hurriedly. "Nobody you would know." The picture quickly disappeared from view.

Grandad who had seen but not heard the incident looked annoyed. "You told me you had thrown that picture away years ago, Lily."

"Well I thought I had. I'll move them all out of the way."

Anxious to change the subject she told the boys there was a box full of family photographs in the spare-room wardrobe. Hardly able to believe his luck Simon rushed off to fetch them.

Simon rummaged through the box carelessly discarding pictures of Aunt Beryl in her first dance dress, out-of-focus holiday snapshots, or anything that did not have an obvious bearing on his quest.

Grandma was poring nostalgically over old wedding pictures, surprised though not displeased by the interest shown by Simon's friend. He wanted to know who everybody was. Even the years of particular fashions. Unusual for a boy. But it was gratifying to have somebody to whom she could explain all the names and relationships. Grandma's memory was a positive encyclopaedia of family events.

It was Morgan who unearthed the picture of a wistful young man in battledress. He held it up inquiringly.

"That is the last photograph of young Frank. My first child. Simon's uncle."

So there had been an elder brother. Both boys looked up expectantly.

"He fought in the North African desert with the Eighth Army. We had a telegram to say he was missing, presumed dead. That was the hardest of all. We went on hoping for so long. . . "

Quickly she lifted up a picture of a smiling, chubby baby. Clearly she did not want to say anything more about Frank. "Debbie was a lovely little thing. So like your Aunt Beryl."

"Who was I like, Grandma?" Simon seized the opportunity.

"Heinz 57 varieties, I think." The response came quickly and brightly.

"Let's find a baby photo of me."

But there was none. The earliest picture of Simon to be found was when he was nearly school age; a family group just after Debbie was born.

Ordinarily Simon would have found all this extremely boring, but today it was quite different. This was time well spent. Grandma supplied them with a family chronicle of who married whom, their jobs, families, where they lived. . .

All valuable information, because it meant that Simon and Morgan could rule out most of the branches of the family in their search for F.C. Grandad's sister, for instance, had had no children. Late in life she had married a ne'er do well who had had the grace to depart early from the scene.

The boys were left with two positive leads, both promising: the moustached young man in the photo frame, and the soldier uncle who had gone missing in the war.

Morgan had even remembered to check out Grandad's hair colour when young. Black.

Grandma agreed to let Simon take away some of the pictures to keep with the family tree he explained he was compiling. One of these was a picture of "young Frank". A happy, laughing snapshot of a young man holding a racquet at a jaunty angle, leaning against the net of a tennis court.

The white disc of the moon was clearly visible in the sky when they glanced through the window as the two boys said their farewells.

"It is not a new moon I hope," commented Grandma. "It's unlucky to look at a new moon through glass."

"If I didn't look at a new moon through glass, I would never see it at all." Morgan adjusted his glasses on his nose. There was no room for superstition in his rational mind.

CHAPTER FOUR

"It is a simple question of not understanding the area and the local issues. They go on bringing people in from other parts of the country for all the senior appointments. I wouldn't care so much if they weren't paid a lot more than me – and then they rely on me to do the work."

The Peppers were having their evening meal. Simon sat eating his shepherd's pie silently, wondering just how many times he had listened to this particular diatribe. There was more to follow – Mr Pepper was not a man of few words – but Simon cut himself off from the stream of talk.

There was probably more than a grain of truth in Mr Pepper's complaint. Simon did not doubt that his father was conscientious, hardworking and capable. And they had watched the pattern repeat itself time and time again as men came in from outside to take executive jobs above his father

Mrs Pepper was making the usual soothing, sympathetic noises. Perhaps she felt a little guilty, thought Simon. Long ago his father had been told that if he wanted promotion he must be prepared to move.

And Simon remembered the endless discussions about whether the family should go here or there as particular jobs fell vacant. At one time Simon believed it might really happen but his mother had always found convincing reasons for staying put. Either they would interrupt the children's schooling, or it would be a shame to leave the house when they had got it just the way they wanted. . . Or, who was going to look after Mr Pepper's parents as they grew older?

The upshot of it all was that they never went. Mr Pepper remained in the same job and it had been a long time since he had even broached the subject of moving.

On this particular evening Simon's mother switched the subject tactfully by inquiring about his visit to his grandparents. Normally he would have been uncommunicative, but on this occasion he seized the opportunity to tell the story of the broken picture frame.

"Well I don't suppose that was much of a loss," commented Mr Pepper. "There must be dozens of photograph frames all over the house. I don't think my mother has ever thrown anything away. I always remember knocking over a ghastly little pink dog, made of chalky stuff, that someone had brought as a present from Southend. It was a genuine accident but I was delighted to see the back of it. But two days later there it was back on the mantelpiece carefully glued together."

Simon was impatient. "There were some other photographs tucked away behind that one." Mr

Pepper nodded – he wasn't surprised. "And one of them really annoyed Grandad. He was furious, and said he thought Grandma had thrown it out years ago."

There was no response in his father's face as Simon described the toothy young man. "Do you know who he was?" He tried to supress the sharpness of his interest.

"I don't know I'm sure. I can't say I have ever felt much interest in all the relatives my mother keeps pictures of. But I can't imagine why any should annoy my father. He has never got involved in family arguments."

"This man had a moustache, a pinstripe suit and a carnation in his buttonhole."

After a few minutes' puzzled contemplation Mr Pepper's face broke into a grin. "Oh, yes. I know who that was. It was the young man my mother was engaged to before she met dad. He was supposed to be rather a dashing, irresponsible character. Too much so for my mother – she didn't like his drinking. So she broke off the engagement and he went to America. I know she kept his photograph. It was a bit of vanity really – particularly when somebody told her he had a big house in California with countless bathrooms and bedrooms, and of course a swimming pool. My father has always been a bit touchy about it."

Simon smiled; he had never thought of his grandparents in that way before, as people who could be jealous and hurt, and perhaps resentful. In fact he had never thought about them much at all, except as old people, set in their ways, preoccupied with warmth, and food, and illness.

Mrs Pepper was bustling around clearing the

table. Simon wanted to raise the subject of the missing brother but his father was clearly getting ready to rush off to the office sports' club.

"Do you want to come and have a game of tennis? It's the junior coaching evening tonight."

Simon didn't feel much like playing tennis but the outing might give him a chance to raise the questions he wanted to ask. Mr Pepper looked highly gratified when he nodded.

"Hurry up and get your things then."

Inevitably that took far longer than intended. Simon had no idea where his plimsolls or shorts were. He also stopped to look for the family tree he had drawn the night before. He thought he had left it on his pillow but his mother must have moved it when she made the bed.

Experience had taught him never to be too dogmatic about where he had left anything. Too often it turned up somewhere else. But the scribbled plan was not to be found anywhere. His father, pacing the hall, called out to him to hurry. Simon grabbed his tennis things and ran.

Mr Pepper was clearly irritated at being kept waiting. They set off to walk briskly to the sports club. "I really don't know how you exist without any sort of system," he muttered.

Systems had a virtue of their own in Mr Pepper's life. Simon half listened as comments about organization, saving time, having a place for everything washed over him. It was hardly an opportune moment to chat about family relationships, he thought sourly.

Privately Simon had long considered that the demands of housework and gardening at 52 Chaucer Road were too rigorously obeyed. Everything had to be done at its appointed time, in its prescribed way. Family outings were fitted around the demands of grass cutting, ironing or washing the kitchen floor. February 19 was firmly imprinted on Simon's mind as the date the tomato seeds *had* to be planted in the greenhouse!

It was either natural inclination or rebellion that made Simon determined to reduce his own bedroom to reassuring chaos. His mother refused to leave it alone. She argued he would never be able to find things if she didn't clear it up. The result was he had nowhere private to keep his own things. That was why his poems were tucked away in old exercise books.

His father's lecture on tidiness and efficiency made Simon's anticipation of the tennis evening plummet even farther. His only hope was that his father would be in an expansive mood on the way home.

CHAPTER FIVE

Tennis whites against the green of the courts made an appealing picture in the evening sun and to his surprise Simon found himself enjoying the game much more than he had expected. He felt quite proud of some of his passing shots even though they were probably more by chance than design.

But that was only until his father appeared on the sidelines. He had been a county tennis player in his youth and his arrival heralded a continuous stream of instructions.

"Run forward to take that ball."

"No. No! You should have seen all that open space at the back there."

"Get it! Leave it! Up to the net! Stay back!" Simon felt more wooden and puppet-like with each order, though the other players were clearly more seriously intent on improving their games. By the time he walked off the court Simon's stomach was knotted with exasperation.

The right way to do things was always crystal

clear to Mr Pepper. He left no room for argument. Simon longed to be allowed to make his own mistakes.

But it was far too beautiful an evening to remain tensed up for long. The air was warm, heavy, and softly scented, and Simon lay on the grass until it was time to go. Lights were just beginning to illuminate the woolly dusk, which wrapped itself round them like a comforting shawl, as Simon and his father started to amble home.

It was the time of day Simon liked best, cosy and optimistic.

"Was your brother good at tennis?" Simon inquired casually. "Grandma let me have a picture of him standing holding a racquet."

Mr Pepper looked surprised. "I didn't know you were interested in the family." He paused. "Everyone on my side of the family seems to have been keen on sport. I don't know about tennis but my brother was just beginning to reach national level in athletics when the war began. . . "

"What was he like?"

"I didn't know him very well. He was eight years older than me. I was only ten when he went into the Army. I think he was probably very like my father, very outgoing and popular. He certainly had lots of friends."

This didn't sound like the red-haired poet, but Simon persisted.

"What did he look like?"

"He was well-built with rather heavy features, and I remember he had very round, staring sort of eyes."

"Was he dark?" Simon already had a good idea from the pictures that he was fair but he was searching for more precise information.

"His hair was a sort of sandy colour. Like my mother's when she was younger."

Could sandy be a sort of red? Simon wondered. "What did he like to read or do apart from sport?"

Mr Pepper was puzzled by the insistent questioning. "Quite honestly I don't know. He had a big stamp collection but he wasn't a bookish type. I know he had a college place waiting for him when he came out of the army. Something to do with maths and accountancy, I think."

Simon felt discouraged. "Young Frank" was beginning to sound more and more like a real Pepper every minute, not an odd ball like himself.

His father's voice became more confidential. "To tell you the truth I never took much interest in my brother. It is probably difficult for you to understand but I resented him after he was lost in the war. My parents were so heartbroken they turned him into a sort of god. I don't think my father ever really got over his death. He gave up his own sport and lost all interest in life. Beryl and I didn't count for anything in his eyes. Everything I did, Frank had done before – only better. It was like living in someone else's shadow. Eventually I think my mother sensed what was happening and tried to make it up to us, but she was having a struggle herself helping my father to pull himself out of his dejection and running the shop at the same time. It would have been so much easier if they had known for sure he was dead. They went on hoping and hoping. . . I used to see my father staring out of the window watching for Frank to stride up the road."

Simon felt a tenderness towards his father that

he had never experienced before. His voice was gentle. "Did they never find a body?"

"No."

"I was trying to draw up a family tree. I'll put him on. I got lots of information from Grandma."

"I think that's an excellent idea." His father was obviously enthusiastic. "It shouldn't be too difficult to find the information because the Peppers have lived around here for generations. I'll give you a hand if you want. My mother should be a mine of information. I can just about remember my father's father, Frank Horace. He was a formidable old man. . . "

The dialogue was interrupted as they reached the back door and went into the kitchen, having to step over the contents of the pantry which were scattered all over the floor. It was being "turned out", part of the ritual whenever guests were expected.

Simon made himself scarce. He had forgotten to go to the library to change his books today. He gazed at the selection in the family bookcase. It was a strange assortment of health, gardening and do-it-yourself manuals, a few paperback thrillers, children's encyclopaedias and a handful of book club titles.

His eye settled on an old adventure story. It must have been his father's. There was a fascination about the embossed picture on the cover of two boys in formal, old-fashioned and quite inappropriate clothes climbing up a haystack.

Simon picked up the book and went upstairs. It had been a pretty negative day. He had written off the toothy young man in his search, and the missing soldier uncle now seemed only a remote possibility.

There was a strong family resemblance between all the Peppers – except him. Simon was more and more convinced that the mystery lay outside his family. He must be adopted. And Debbie? He had heard of couples who had adopted a child because they thought they couldn't have children only to find later they had a baby of their own after all.

Somewhere in his background there was something shameful and embarrassing, something the Peppers didn't want him to know. Far from being appalled he was rather attracted to the idea.

Simon lay back on his bed and opened the book. In a bold and flowing hand was the name Frank Charles Pepper. From Mother and Dad, Christmas 1936.

The initials jumped out at Simon. F.C. His imagination made enormous leaps. Perhaps he wasn't lost in the war. Could he have deserted? Had he disgraced himself in some way? The Peppers were an intensely proud family. Was this the reason they were so heartbroken? Had they begun to weave a "tangled web" of lies around their missing son to cover their shame?

CHAPTER SIX

Mrs Pepper's preparations for Jenny and Pop's visit were beginning to reach an all time high. Simon arrived downstairs rather late to find some breakfast things laid out on a tray.

Investigating bumping and scraping noises in Debbie's bedroom Simon discovered his mother trying to hump out furniture in order to roll back the carpet.

"When you've had your breakfast can you come and give me a hand to move the heavier things?" she asked breathlessly. "I want to paint the room to have it fresh and clean before Jenny and Pop come."

"I thought Dad usually did that," Simon commented ungraciously.

"He is far too busy at the office at the moment. I can manage all right if I have some help move the furniture."

Simon agreed to help but he felt quite out of sympathy with the venture. He looked round Debbie's room. There was nothing at all wrong with it as far as he could see.

In any case he didn't suppose for a moment Jenny and Pop would be crawling around looking for scratch marks on the skirting board.

His mother read his thoughts. "If we waited until you noticed something was wrong we would be living in a pigsty." A pigsty might be more fun, Simon thought uncharitably.

He felt uneasy eating breakfast while his mother was waiting for his help. Nevertheless he sat over a cup of tea reading the newspaper as a way of registering his disapproval.

His loyalties were divided. He knew he should offer to do some of the painting; on the other hand he had arranged to see Morgan to work out their plan of campaign.

The door bell rang. It was the milkman wanting payment of the bill.

"Mum," Simon yelled upstairs, "the milkman wants his money."

"I can't come now. Find my bag and pay him for me please."

Simon located the bag and took the purse across to the milkman. There was not quite enough silver. He went back to get the wallet and searched through a variety of pockets. He unzipped one part and looked in. No money there. Just a piece of paper. There was something familiar about the paper. He started. Yes, it was the family tree he had drawn – carefully put away.

The milkman jingled his money bag impatiently. Simon found a note and handed it over. He took the change without looking at it.

His body felt on edge, like a violin tuned to its highest pitch. Now there was absolutely no doubt in his mind that there was some secret in his family background. Why else the carefully hidden piece of paper? Did his mother want to discuss it with his father? He carefully replaced the paper in its original pocket.

"Simon are you coming? I can't get on until I have moved the wardrobe."

His mother was bustling around full of nervous energy. He looked at her closely as they fetched and carried. Slim and small, she was forever baking and cooking but Simon had never known his mother put on an extra pound in weight. Her features were delicate and even, but around the eyes and mouth there were unmistakeable signs of tension.

There was seldom any real friction between his parents: it wasn't a home where there were many rows and yet for a long time Simon had sensed that his mother was anxious and unhappy. What it was all about he could not guess.

"I have a message for you, Simon." His mother's voice was hesitant and rather remote. "Mr Marchington phoned earlier. Now he has retired he has started work on a book of children's poems, and he wondered if you would like to take round some of the poems you've written, and help him sort out some of the others."

Simon was delighted. He looked quickly at his mother. Her face was mask-like.

"Have you got many poems, Simon?" She was clearly trying to sound detached. "A few."

Both were on their guard. "I'll go round to Mr Marchington's later. I promised to go to Morgan's this morning."

His mother nodded silently and turned her attention to the emulsion paint.

CHAPTER SEVEN

"Draw another family tree around only the Pepper family and see if your mother shows any interest in that."

The boys were sitting in the room Morgan shared with Evan. Morgan hurled a tee shirt across the room. He strove to maintain some degree of order in his "half", unceremoniously tossing back his younger brother's possessions as they spilled into his part.

"I think our man is far more likely to be on her side of the family," he commented sagely. He wrote off Frank Charles Pepper and the desertion theory as only a remote possibility. The tennis racquet photo suggested no obvious resemblance.

"I don't think your father is the sort to fabricate stories. Now your mother is different. Much deeper and more secretive."

Simon bristled. However much he criticized his own parents he resented anybody else doing it, however slightly. Nevertheless Morgan's arguments were convincing. His friend's earlier scepticism had evaporated, and now he was as certain as Simon that there was a mystery to be unravelled.

It was the absence of baby photos which had tipped the scales as far as Morgan was concerned. For a family so eager to chronicle their events he was mystified by the lack of pictures of Simon as a baby. "Our problem is that we are pursuing too many avenues at once. We are fighting on two fronts. The adoption theory *and* the disgraced relative in the family tree. We have somehow got to establish first and foremost whether you are adopted before we get too involved with the family tree."

"There are problems with the adoption theory," Morgan went on solemnly. "Your parents have been married for nearly sixteen years – actually it is their anniversary very soon."

"How on earth do you know that?" Simon interrupted.

Morgan couldn't disguise a certain degree of smugness. "I asked your grandmother when we were looking at the wedding photos. That means they were married about two years before you were born, which makes it very unlikely they adopted you because they couldn't have children of their own. My mother said people usually have to wait several years before they can adopt a baby. And usually they have been married for years before they realize they can't have children."

Morgan had clearly being doing his homework. Or more precisely questioning his mother.

"Sometimes when an unmarried girl in the family has a baby one of the other relatives brings it up," said Simon.

They thought around that idea for a while. Aunt Beryl had to be ruled out; she must have been married longer than Simon's parents as two of Simon's cousins were older than him. Nobody else seemed to fit the bill.

Morgan took a piece of paper. "You had better draw up your new family tree soon." He was making a list of their tasks. "Put in Frank Charles Pepper and see what response it gets."

"There is the question of blood groups," Simon volunteered. "I'll try asking this evening. This afternoon I've got to see Marchington."

He explained about the schoolmaster's call.

"I'm going to the library this afternoon so I'll try to get something on tracing one's family tree," said Morgan.

They felt rather pleased with their progress and settled down to a game of chess.

CHAPTER EIGHT

Simon had never been to Mr Marchington's house before but he knew well enough where he lived. It was an old terraced house very near the school.

Mr Marchington's beaky face was surmounted by a mop of white hair and this together with his gruff, strict manner always intimidated the first-year new boys. However he was the Mr Chips of the high school, taking pains to seek out and try to help those boys with problems, who didn't seem to be achieving what he knew they should.

Simon had long intrigued him. He had no doubt that the boy had a rare imagination and great ability in English but something held him back at school. He had been surprised when he had talked to the parents at a school evening. They certainly wanted Simon to do well, but the master sensed they had little appreciation of his real though rather individual talents.

He remained quiet when Simon told him about his mother's reaction to his winning the poetry prize. The boy did not elaborate, and the old schoolmaster had learned not to pry. He waited for boys to tell him their confidences in their own time.

Together the two spent a happy and busy afternoon sifting through poems. Mr Marchington sought, and clearly respected, Simon's opinions on some of the poems he was doubtful about, and several of Simon's own poems had been included in the bundle of manuscripts to be dispatched to the publishers.

Mr Marchington was going to take the papers with him when he went away on holiday to the cottage he had bought to retire to. He had often described the cottage to his pupils. He had paid very little for it. It was part of the coastline which was being steadily eaten away by the sea, and already the main village lay under the water but Mr Marchington was sure the cottage would last him out his days.

Over a cup of tea Mr Marchington quizzed Simon about how he came to write poetry. But Simon could not explain it. It was like an inner compulsion rather than anything he ever set out deliberately to do.

All he knew was that he could only write when he was quite alone, cut off from the rest of the world. Then his complete absorption often eased the painful feeling of isolation that sometimes came over him. But this was far too private for him to talk to anybody about – even Mr Marchington.

As Simon walked home later that afternoon he luxuriated in a warm glow of contentment at the schoolmaster's genuine gratitude for his help. He had said he would call again early in September when Mr Marchington returned from his seaside spell.

The piercing shrill of an ambulance siren made him jump and reminded him that he had to tackle the question of his blood group some time that evening. He had drawn up a new family tree based on the information given by Grandma Pepper. He must remember to show it to his parents.

Mrs Pepper was trying to ease the toad-in-the-hole out of the dish when Simon raised the subject of his blood group. She stopped in surprise at his words.

"I thought I would buy a St Christopher pendant," he began. "The sort with a secret pocket at the back where you can write all sorts of medical information, you know like your blood group and whether you have any serious illnesses."

"But you haven't – I hope," his mother commented, superstitiously touching the wooden table, astounded that Simon would consider wearing jewellery. He never even changed his clothes unless she removed the ones he was wearing from his bedroom.

"It doesn't exactly seem you," she commented cautiously. "But your birthday is coming up soon we could give you one then."

"Well I'll let you know about that very soon," said Simon hastily. He quite categorically did not want a pendant. He had never heard of such a thing until Morgan had mentioned it after a visitor had called at their house sporting one. The last thing Simon wanted was that what he thought was a subtle ploy should rebound on himself in the shape of an embarrassing and actively unwanted birthday present.

"I really think it would be a good idea if I knew my blood group," Simon persisted. "Just in case of an accident."

"You haven't had any cabbage, Simon." His mother was reproachful. She didn't like such conversations. Simon loathed cabbage but he took a small portion. The whole family knew how much emphasis Mrs Pepper placed on the health-giving properties of fresh vegetables.

"It is something I should know," Simon was determined not to be sidetracked.

"Why?" Mr Pepper amused himself and irritated his family by appearing deliberately blank on occasions.

"Well, I might need a transfusion. If I was in a really bad accident it would be a waste of time if they had to analyse my blood first. It could be a matter of life and death."

Mr Pepper was laconic. "I should have thought that if it was such a serious accident you would not be in a position to tell them your blood group. Even if you knew it."

"That is the point of the pendant." Simon said with growing apprehension that his mother might take the argument too seriously and insist he wore such a piece of jewellery!

"Well I have no idea what it is." His father concluded the discussion flatly.

"What is yours? That'd give me a clue." Simon looked carefully at his parents' faces.

"Simon, don't let your meal get cold," his mother chided.

"As a matter of fact, I do know mine," Mr Pepper announced helpfully. "I used to be a blood donor. I was in the commonest group of all, O.

There is no blue blood about us, I'm afraid."

Mrs Pepper had no recollection of her group but she did remember having a hospital card on which it was marked. That would be in her husband's carefully filed system of family information. In the face of Simon's persistence his father agreed to look for it after the meal.

He handed over the card for Simon's inspection. There was the name of the local hospital, his mother's name, Mrs C. Pepper and the category of her blood group, O Rhesus positive. Just like his father's.

"That should simplify things a bit," said his father. "You must be O too."

"Unless," Simon looked at his father closely, "it can skip a generation of two. Like my red hair."

Mr Pepper was thoughtful. "Perhaps," he nodded. He took back the card and was clearly unwilling to be drawn further.

"Would you like to see the family tree so far?"

"Certainly as long as it won't take long. There is a programme I want to watch in ten minutes."

Simon bounded up to his room and burst into the living room with the paper which he handed to his father as casually as he could.

Mrs Pepper looked up from the newspaper. "What is that, Simon?"

"It's the family tree I've drawn up."

"Oh!" There was a catch in his mother's voice. "What gave you the idea of doing that, then?"

She had put down the paper and went over to where his father was sitting. She leant over his shoulder and looked at the sheet.

"Oh! it is the Peppers," she commented. Simon detected a note of relief in her voice.

Unconcerned his mother returned to her chair.

"I'll do your family next," Simon commented. "Perhaps Jenny and Pop could fill me in a bit when they come."

"I shouldn't bother about that," said his mother very quickly. "It's usual just to trace the main line on the father's side. After all, the female lines keep changing their names."

She added: "Besides, the Peppers have lived round here for generations so it will be a lot easier for you to find out about them. My family have moved around a lot."

"Your mother's right. Concentrate on the Peppers. It is much easier to follow one name through first."

Mr Pepper studied the paper. "It looks pretty accurate to me. You'll soon know more about the family than I do."

Simon secretly doubted the accuracy of that comment. But his parents' approval of this particular line of inquiry made him more and more convinced that the answer to his quest did *not* lie within the Pepper family.

CHAPTER NINE

Simon often wished that Morgan was not quite so thorough. Not only had his friend visited the library and acquired a copy of *Tracing Your Ancestors* but he had spotted a notice for blood donors to go to St Mark's church hall that very afternoon.

Morgan was bright and bossy about it all. "You must go. They have to tell you your particular group. If it turns out you're the same as your parents we'll scotch the adoption theory and concentrate on the undesirable relative."

Simon felt slightly sick. A vision of long, tiled hospital corridors reeking with disinfectant swept over him. "I don't fancy it, at all." He shuddered. "Would you come along too?"

He clutched at the idea of moral support.

"Sorry," Morgan tried unsuccessfully to sound disappointed. "They are short of people in the Baptist chapel choir and Mum arranged with the minister for Madoc and I to go along. We've got to see him this afternoon."

It was the first time Morgan had felt any pleasure in his mother's suggestion.

"We have to go to practices every Thursday evening if we join."

Simon had no interest at all in the Baptist chapel choir. He was far too concerned about going to St Mark's Hall.

"Oh, well," he concluded gloomily, "I suppose I had better go."

By lunchtime Simon's legs had developed a strange feeling of weakness. He pushed away his fish fingers and chips.

Mrs Pepper looked concerned. "What's the matter, Simon. Have you got an upset stomach?"

"I'm all right. I just don't feel like food."

He left the table. Unsure what being a blood donor was or what part of the anatomy was involved, he decided to have a precautionary all-over wash before setting off on his expedition. He felt that the occasion called for clean underwear and duly changed his clothes. His half-hour occupation of the bathroom – a rare event for Simon – followed by his neat and clean appearance mystified Mrs Pepper.

"Going anywhere special?"

"Just into town."

Simon's dislike of shopping was well-known in the family. When he really needed new clothes Mrs Pepper usually bought the articles "on spec" and had to trail back to the shop with them if they did not fit.

"Are you going shopping?"

"No."

St Mark's Hall was an incredible building. Its façade was covered with tiles, and it was decorated with small towers and shapes looking like a bad copy of something someone had once seen in the Orient.

Simon stepped through the doors. A heavily-built woman in a business-like white overall sat at a desk near the entrance surrounded by a collection of filing cabinets, in-trays and out-trays. The rest of the hall was obscured by screens. A nurse appeared from behind a screen and handed a paper to the woman at the desk who looked up at Simon, raising her eyebrows questioningly.

"I want to be a blood donor."

"Well it's very nice of you to offer but we never take blood from children."

"I'm thirteen, nearly fourteen", he pointed out, "that's old enough to decide whether I want to give blood."

"I'm sorry," the woman insisted. "But we couldn't possibly consider it without your parents' consent."

"That is ridiculous. It's my body. Nobody can stop me if I want to jump off a high wall and break my bones."

"I hope," she said stiffly, "you do not do anything as foolish as that."

"I am not trying to do anything foolish. Perhaps I might save a few lives. How do you know," he said passionately warming to his subject, "that somebody is not going to die because you did not take my blood?"

"I shouldn't worry about that. Hospitals have reasonable supplies of all the main groups."

"But I might be one of the rare groups, and you will need all you can get if there is a terrible plane crash or a train comes off the rails." Simon's imagination was becoming more and more gory, secure in the knowledge that the purposeful lady could not be swayed in her decision.

"What group do you think you are?"

"I don't know. That's the point."

The nurse arrived with another piece of paper.

"Look," said the woman decisively. "We don't normally have offers from children. I haven't come across it before. If you are very eager to help us you must get your mother or father to telephone our regional headquarters and ask for their advice."

She wrote a telephone number on a piece of paper and handed it to Simon. He was dismissed.

CHAPTER TEN

Mrs Pepper bustled in from her Thursday afternoon meeting. "Simon," she called as she stooped down to put a casserole in the oven.

Simon, who was half-heartedly tackling a bit of holiday homework in his room, came downstairs.

"I have just been to my guild meeting."

He waited. After what Mrs Pepper felt was a significant pause, she continued.

"Mrs Henderson was there."

She looked for some response from Simon. Feeling he ought to contribute something to the conversation he said "Oh," followed by "I don't know Mrs Henderson."

"Well, she certainly knows you," his mother continued. "She is our guild secretary, but on Wednesdays," she paused for effect, "she is the nurse at the blood donors' centre."

Simon flushed.

"I don't understand it Simon. What has got into you? Half the time I can't get you to the doctor's surgery but Mrs Henderson said that you were most persistent about wanting to give blood."

"Well," said Simon defensively, "giving blood is a worthwhile thing to do. After all, Dad did it when he was younger."

"There are many worthwhile things to do," commented his mother, "but you do not seem to feel you need to do most of them."

"Well," continued Simon, "I thought they would tell me my blood group. It's just something I want to know."

"You're developing an obsession about accidents," his mother remarked. "It would be more to the point if you stopped day-dreaming when you were riding your bicycle rather than bothering about your blood group."

Mrs Pepper started pottering about the kitchen. Simon assumed that the matter was closed and started to walk back to his room.

"But Mrs Henderson is a very good-hearted woman."

Simon turned back.

"She said if you were only bothered about your blood group you could go along next Wednesday afternoon and she would find out what it was for you."

Morgan was in the kitchen experimenting with his chemistry set when Simon called a week later to tell him the result of his blood test. As it turned out it had proved far less of an ordeal than he had expected. Little more than a pin prick in fact. Mrs Thomas, clad in a dramatic full-length dress in scarlet and black, led Simon through the house.

"Go and clean your teeth," she called out to

Evan and Llewellyn.

"I'm taking them to the dentist," she explained in a friendly way to Simon as she opened the kitchen door.

Morgan was bending over a few test tubes perched on a small area of the draining board – the only corner of the kitchen not already occupied. A giant jar of honey, which Mrs Thomas had bought in bulk, occupied the rest of the draining board, while the family hamster's cage stood on a nearby surface, its owner vigorously occupied in tearing newspaper pieces to shreds.

The two small Thomas boys quickly reappeared. Their mother inspected their teeth.

"Right! We're off now," she announced, cheerfully oblivious of dirty knees, untied shoelaces and holey sweaters. "We'd better take some games in case we are held up."

Simon looked around the kitchen for something to sit on. The only stool held a pile of clothes waiting to be ironed.

Morgan had half filled a test-tube with water. "Hold this!" he said. "I've got to put a bit of litmus paper in it. Litmus, litmus. . . here it is!"

Simon held the tube while Morgan attempted to add a small quantity of the powder. He tipped up the tube of powder too sharply and a large quantity of blue powder dropped into the test-tube, water splashing on to the floor.

"Bother." Morgan tipped some of the inky blue liquid down the sink.

"I've got the result of my blood test."

Morgan was fumbling for matches trying to light a small spirit lamp. He stopped and looked up with interest. "Well?"

"It's O Rhesus positive."

Morgan nodded and resumed his experiment.

"Go and look in the pantry for some vinegar, lemon juice, washing soda and ammonia," he asked, reading from the list in the book.

Simon walked into the large pantry. It was hard to know where to start. There were packets, tins and jars of all sorts. A bowl of goldfish stood on the tiled surface and a greasy tennis ball occupied a white plate. Eventually he located a squeezy lemon and a jar of pickled cabbage.

"We can use the liquid from the pickles," he explained, pleased with his own enterprise. Ammonia and washing soda he located beneath the sink.

"Put some lemon into the tube."

Simon obliged. The dark blue liquid turned reddy orange. "Acid," said Morgan with satisfaction.

"Are you disappointed about your blood test?" his friend inquired as an afterthought.

"It's hard to say," answered Simon truthfully. "In a way I am and in a way I'm not." There were times when he genuinely wanted to belong to his family. And times when he most positively did not.

They continued adding things to the solution. A smell of vinegar and ammonia began to fill the kitchen and trails of colourful liquid spread around the place. Morgan systematically ticked off the experiments as they were completed. He spoke little.

"All these are alkalis because they turn the litmus blue," he announced. "But when you think about it the litmus doesn't show which alkali they are."

It did not seem a very interesting problem to Simon. "So? They look different. You can see what they are."

"Yes," Morgan said. "The test proves they're alkalis, but it doesn't prove which alkali they are. Your blood test is like that."

Simon looked mystified. Morgan was slightly impatient.

"If your parents had not been group O the Peppers wouldn't have been your parents." Simon nodded. "But if you are group O it showed they could be your parents, but it does not prove they are," he announced triumphantly.

Simon still looked puzzled.

"Group O is quite common isn't it?"

"About half the population are O," Simon agreed. He had gleaned the information from an encyclopaedia.

"Well then," announced Morgan, "if you were adopted there would still be a one in two chance that you would be group O anyway."

Simon groaned. "I see. But that takes us right back to the beginning again."

Morgan's face gave little away. He was concentrating on tipping bits of logwood into a test-tube, scattering an equal amount on the draining board. He began to repeat the whole process of experiments. It was not long before Mrs Thomas returned.

"That looks exciting," she commented pleasantly, apparently unconcerned about the powerful smells or the pools of red, orange and blue liquid which were being tramped around the kitchen.

She started buttering scones on top of the cooker. "Staying to tea, Pep?" she inquired.

"No, I'd better not, thank you," he replied. "I'll have to get along soon." He was beginning to find the smell of the experiments very unpleasant.

Mrs Thomas was spooning honey from the gigantic jar.

"Oh, Morgan, while I remember it, there won't be a choir practice this week. I heard while I was out that the minister's wife has had her baby. So Mr Davies will be going to the hospital and he won't be able to take the practice tonight."

"Good," said Morgan.

Mrs Thomas appeared not to notice.

"It was a boy," she chattered on. "I knew it would be because it was three weeks late and boys are often late in arriving. You four all kept us waiting a couple of weeks or so."

"Mmm," Morgan acknowledged her remarks without any visible interest, "I'll come to the end of the road with you," he said turning to Simon.

"I've had another idea," he said as they strolled along. "Oh," said Simon.

"You know what my mother was saying about boys arriving late and all that sort of thing," Morgan said waving his hand distastefully, "well, you could ask your mother whether you were born late, or whether you had lots of hair when you were born or cried a lot. You know the sort of things people ask about babies." Morgan was anxious not to seem too knowledgeable on the subject.

"Mmm." There was little enthusiasm in Simon's voice. Day dreams were one thing. But real life detective quests were proving very frustrating and negative. He would rather escape to his own world of the imagination and leave the practical realities to someone else.

Not so Morgan. He had got the scent of the chase and was determined to keep Simon on course.

CHAPTER ELEVEN

Simon sat back, eating happily, basking in the warm, family atmosphere. Mrs Pepper poured tea from the elegant silver teapot that had been in Jenny's family for generations. Its slender lines and delicately engraved design always delighted Simon.

The table was spread festively for a special tea to mark Jenny and Pop's arrival. There was a lively, excited buzz of chatter and everyone was constantly interrupted by Debbie's offers of food.

Jenny looked as lady-like as ever in her pale blue perfectly matched outfit which complemented her gently waved white hair. Simon always noticed that his grandmother smelled nice. Perhaps it was her powder. Pop, a strongly-built man in his seventies, had a jaunty air in his new lightweight summer suit.

As the first flood of chatter began to subside Jenny put her hand in her handbag and produced two small packages wrapped in tissue paper. "I bought the children rather different gifts from usual," she explained. "Pop and I thought they had all the toys and things they could want, and anyway Simon is getting too old for that kind of thing, so I thought I would give each of you something that belonged to your great grandparents."

Jenny carefully handed over a package to each child. Debbie shrieked with delight as she opened hers. It was a silver pendant necklace. A turquoise green stone gleamed in a setting decorated with delicate silver tracery as fragile-looking as a spider's web. She rushed over to her mother, eager to have it fastened round her neck.

Simon looked down at his gift, a gold fob watch which shone in the palm of his hand. The most marvellous present he had ever received. He said nothing for a few minutes.

Jenny came over to him. "It does work if you wind the knob."

"It is absolutely beautiful," said Simon quietly. It was something he would treasure always. He fingered the heavy gold chain which must have rested in the top pocket of his great grandfather's jacket. The whole watch was elaborately worked and decorated. In the centre of the elegant black Roman numerals on its gold face was an intricately worked pattern of rose leaves. The back of the watch had been worn smooth with use, but the pattern of flowers, leaves and twirling shapes was still clearly distinguishable.

Jenny showed him how to put his nail on the tiny catch which released the hands of the watch and allowed them to be set at the correct time. Simon wound up the watch with great care, anxious not to strain or damage it in any way. Nothing could have given him greater pleasure.

Debbie was the centre of attention excitedly showing off her silver necklace. But Jenny sat quietly by Simon's side.

"You'll take care of that watch, won't you Simon?" she asked in a gentle voice. "It is one of the few things I have that belonged to my father. I've been keeping it for you because you are the first boy in the family since him. My father always wanted a son and he had two girls. I am sure he would be pleased to know that his great grandson had his watch."

Simon assured his grandmother that he would take the greatest care of his watch and he really meant it. It would be his most precious possession.

There were games that night, family games of cards and Monopoly. Later as he lay on the camp bed in the downstairs front room he held the gold watch to his ear listening to the quick, staccato ticking. He looked at the time, 10.30 p.m. Simon wondered whether his great grandfather would have been in bed at that time. He tried to picture the room in which he might have slept. Heavily furnished and dark. A new, reassuring sense of belonging to his family swept over Simon. He had always felt very close to Jenny. She loved him uncritically, accepting him as the person he was. And if he was adopted then he couldn't really claim Jenny or her father as his own. Tonight he realized for the first time just how important this was to him. He wanted to believe that the man who had worn this watch in his top pocket was his great grandfather.

Doubts and confusions evaporated in a warm comfortable sense of family as Simon drifted towards sleep.

CHAPTER TWELVE

But it didn't take long to dispel that comfortable sense of belonging. Every now and then he kicked the turf aggressively as he walked along the river-side with Jenny. "Don't be upset, Simon," her voice was coaxing. Normally she took a rest in the afternoon but today she had suggested going for a walk.

"I wanted to give you this so you could buy another present." She stretched out her hand with a pound note.

Simon froze. "No. I don't want to. Thanks all the same. It isn't just because of this morning. It's everything."

Simon's feelings were too near the surface for him to be able to disguise the rawness of his emotions. He couldn't do anything to please his mother. All he had wanted was to get his parents an anniversary present.

It was at breakfast time, when he had seen the present and card from Jenny and Pop, that he had remembered. He had decided to go to the local shops to buy a gift, and generously had asked Debbie if she wanted him to get something for her to give their parents as well.

Of course she wanted to go too. Mrs Pepper had fussed. Debbie wasn't allowed to cycle to the shops. When she finally agreed to let Debbie go, she gave Simon strict instructions about looking after his sister.

When they arrived at the shops Debbie had insisted on buying chocolates. Simon hadn't much idea what he could get his parents until he spotted an off-licence. A bottle of wine: that was an idea.

"Wait here," he told Debbie firmly, leaving her outside the shop. It took some time. And when the assistant had pointed out that he shouldn't be buying anything alcoholic at all, it had taken a lot of persuasion before she agreed reluctantly to let him buy a bottle of Sport Cocktail.

He had come out of the shop to find, to his horror, that Debbie had vanished. He had tossed the bottle into his cycle basket and searched up and down the high street for his sister. There was no sign of her.

He went home fearfully, hoping against hope she had gone back ahead of him. "You'll have to go back and find her," said his mother, white-faced with anxiety and putting on her own coat at the same time. "You know she is not big enough to be let alone on the main road."

The morning disintegrated into a nightmare. In and out of shops Simon went, asking if they had seen Debbie. No one could remember her. Up and down the roads that led into the high street he cycled, time and time again. Not a sign of her.

Fear began to escalate. He found himself offering up all sorts of promises in return for his sister's safety. Finally defeated and emotionally spent he cycled slowly home.

He was greeted by sunshine and smiles at Chaucer Road, and his mother, Jenny and Debbie were laughing and chattering. Simon sank down on a stool, limp with relief. No one had thought to come out and look for him. His mother showed little concern about his feelings, only relief that Debbie had been found safe and sound. The little girl had gone off to play at the home of a friend she had spotted in the high street. So delighted was Mrs Pepper at the return of her daughter it was obvious she had not even scolded the child.

It was very clear, Simon thought bitterly, why there were no baby photos of him. His mother cared so much more for Debbie.

Mrs Pepper was touched by the gift of chocolates from Debbie. But when Debbie reminded him to bring in his own anniversary present Simon discovered that in his anxiety he had not propped up his bike properly. It lay sprawled across the pathway, the bottle of Sport Cocktail smashed to pieces. He looked at the spilled liquid with uncertain feelings. He was in no mood to give presents.

Jenny quite understood Simon's refusal to accept her offer to replace the gift; she could imagine how he was feeling. Inwardly she was deeply worried about the boy, but she had resolved long ago never to interfere in Chrissie's family.

She put her hand on Simon's arm. He looked at her with a mixture of hurt and gratitude. "Would you imagine," the words blurted out, "that my mother would be so upset about a poetry prize?"

Jenny picked her words very carefully. "It is very hard for me to say. Your mother feels things very deeply but she can't bring herself to talk about them. It would be so much easier if she let things come to the surface. But that is not the way she is. Even when she was little she would always run away and hide if she was upset."

They were characteristics Simon could identify with, even though Jenny's remarks threw no revealing light on his mother's reasoning. "She's so different with Debbie. She isn't always finding fault with her."

Privately Jenny agreed, but she deflected Simon's comment. "It is hard being the older one," she agreed. "My father was always much stricter with me than my younger sister. She was much prettier too and that made it worse. She could get away with anything. I never could."

"What happened to her?"

"She was killed during the war." Jenny changed the subject. "My father always seemed to find us such a trouble. I suppose it was hard for him to bring up two girls on his own, but when Chrissie was born he was totally different – playing with her and spoiling her. Perhaps it's more fun being a grandparent!" She smiled at him. "You can show your feelings more. My father was a very strong willed old man but Chrissie adored him, and of course she named you after him. Simon Jonathan." She said the name slowly.

The remark brought Simon up with a jolt. He did recall being told that he had been named after his great grandfather. The information had not interested him at the time. Now it provided another small piece of the jigsaw he was trying to fit together.

The gold watch, this feeling of family likeness, his own name. . . knitted together to form one part of the picture. But he no longer had any doubts that there was another vital part of the jigsaw that the rest of the family was trying to hide.

CHAPTER THIRTEEN

A special anniversary tea was waiting when Simon and Jenny returned home. Mr Pepper had arrived ahead of them and was looking at the iced cake and the bottle of Sport Cocktail which stood next to it. Simon realized that his mother must have slipped down to the shops to replace the ill-fated gift.

Simon brought us the cocktail and Debbie the chocolates," she explained. His mother obviously wanted to forget the morning's trouble and was trying to behave as though nothing had gone wrong. Simon was equally happy to do so and the family sat down cheerfully to tea.

Mr Pepper gave everyone a glass, Simon and Debbie included. He poured out the cocktail and Pop proposed a special toast, "To Chrissie and Cyril, wishing them many more years of happiness."

"Ugh!" Debbie pulled a dreadful face and ran straight out into the kitchen. Simon with greater dignity, succeeded in swallowing his glassful but didn't accept the offer of a refill!

All through tea Simon noticed that his father had a slightly impatient, expectant air as if he had something important to say. Mr Pepper had always been an easy person to read.

Sure enough he finally burst into the conversation. "I was in the chief executive's office this afternoon when he told me there was a job in Rockbury that he thought I should apply for." There was both excitement and pride in his father's voice.

Rockbury was a town some thirty to forty kilometres away. A shadow crossed Mrs Pepper's face. "What about the extension?" she asked quickly. "The builders have just begun work on it. And the high school?"

"Well," said Mr Pepper a trifle less confidently, "I could drive there each day if we didn't want to move. But it is a pleasant place and there are some very attractive villages round about. As for the high school. . . "

"That doesn't matter at all," interposed Simon decisively. "I haven't started the O-level syllabus yet, and I don't mind moving at all. Mr Marchington is leaving and he is the only teacher who is any good."

Mrs Pepper was not to be reassured. "It would cost an awful lot to commute, and we would have to get a more reliable car if you were going to travel that sort of mileage. Mrs Scott was telling me the other day it would cost them about £1,000 to sell their house and move. You would need a big rise to cover it either way."

Simon didn't allow his hopes to rise. Already the defences were being raised to keep them firmly in

Chaucer Road. And there would be plenty more to come. His father was looking a little less eager when a surprising ally stepped into the discussion.

"I should give it a try, Chrissie. After all you have been here a long time, and Cyril has reached the stage where he probably wants a new challenge. I know you have got this house nice but you could do just the same somewhere else." There was a pause. "It might blow a few cobwebs away and give you all a new start."

Simon could hardly believe his ears. Jenny who had never interfered or expressed a controversial opinion in his home was arguing quite strongly for a move.

"I'll send in the application form at any rate." Jenny's words had clearly bolstered up Mr Pepper's determination. Simon knew his father admired his mother-in-law and was always anxious to please her. Towards his own parents he was a kind and dutiful son but Jenny and Pop commanded respect. Simon wasn't sure why. Perhaps it was Jenny's lady-like gentility that had won him over or tales of earlier days when the family were much grander than they were now.

Mrs Pepper was still looking rather drawn and preoccupied when the time came to cut the special iced anniversary cake.

Everyone took a piece except Pop.

"You must have a piece too, Pop," cried Debbie.

"I'd love to," he said, "but it is much too rich for me."

"You're not ill," the little girl persisted.

"No, I'm not," he agreed, "but I must be careful what I eat."

"Oh, go on Pop!" Debbie pestered, offering him

a piece. "Just this once."

"Debbie, put that down and leave Pop alone," her father ordered sternly.

Debbie, unused to being scolded, sat down crestfallen, her bottom lip trembling.

"Look Debbie," said Pop, putting his hand under her chin to raise her face, "don't get upset about it. It is just that I have something called sugar diabetes which means that I can't eat sugar. I'm very lucky really because otherwise I'm very healthy. I just have a special injection each day and then I'm as right as rain."

At the mention of the word "injection", Simon and Debbie both winced.

"I hope I don't inherit it," said Simon tactlessly pausing for a moment in the middle of eating his second helping of cake. "I would hate to go without sugar."

"You are quite safe. There's no danger of that. You couldn't get it from me," said Pop slowly and deliberately.

"Why not?" Simon asked quickly.

Jenny and his mother both looked up sharply.

Pop raised his head to answer in his slow, deliberate manner but before he had time to speak Mrs Pepper intervened. "I don't think it is something you can inherit. But let's not talk about medical things at the table."

Simon mulled over the finality of Pop's reply. How could he be so sure his grandson would not have the same trouble? Pop was a cautious, thoughtful character, certainly not given to wildly inaccurate statements.

But it was all forgotten in the discussion about Mr Pepper's possible new job.

It was hours later, when Simon was lying wakefully in bed, that he remembered his grandfather's words. "You can't get it from me." What did he mean? Simon sat up. Because he was sleeping downstairs the bookcase and the family's medical encyclopaedia were just a couple of feet away.

Simon padded across to the door and put on the light. "Dia. . . something." It did not take long to find the entry. That was it. Diabetes. Simon shuddered slightly as he read a list of medical technicalities. No, he would rather not know about it.

His eyes scanned the text quickly. He was just about to close the book when his attention was caught by the words: "Often inherited, particularly through the male line."

CHAPTER FOURTEEN

Morgan was opening and shutting drawers in his room. It was his concession to packing for the family's annual trek to Wales. He had little interest in the packing or the holiday. Right now he was far more concerned about Pop's diabetes.

"What we don't know," he said, "is whether he said that just to reassure you. After all, there is no point in worrying about whether you are going to get something – at least not until you do."

Simon, sprawled on Morgan's bed, considered the problem. "He didn't sound as if he was trying to be reassuring. He seemed quite positive about it."

"Perhaps then you are right and he isn't your grandfather," Morgan concluded slowly.

"Yes but what about the fact that Jenny said I was named after her father, and I was the first boy in the family since then?" Simon fingered the fob watch in his jacket pocket. He was reluctant to give up Jenny and Pop.

"Do you think Jenny is telling the truth?"

"I think," said Simon carefully, " that there are things she doesn't tell me but I don't think Jenny would lie."

"Perhaps what she is not telling you is that she has been married twice and her first husband was the red-haired poet." said Morgan in a flash of inspiration.

Jenny and a red-haired poet? "Mm, well I'll try to find out," Simon agreed doubtfully. "I'm going back with them tomorrow for a holiday."

"Find out how long ago they were married. If it was after your mother was born then her father would be the red-haired poet."

A new idea occurred to Morgan. "What about Jenny's sister? She could have had a red-haired son who wrote poetry and became the black sheep of the family."

Simon weighed up the possibility. "Not if I am the first boy in the family since Simon Jonathan. He would have given the other boy the watch."

"Oh," he added, "I did ask about the baby bit. Mum was quite happy to talk about it. In fact she went on and on. Apparently I was ten days' late, had lots of hair and cried all the time. Dad was knocking on doors in the middle of the night to try to find the midwife."

"I don't suppose she would make all that up," mused Morgan. "No. You will have to concentrate on Jenny and Pop. Find out all you can while you are there. Then somehow or other you and I have to organize a trip to London. . . "

Simon stared at his grandparents across the train carriage. They sat nodding over their paperbacks.

Jenny, in her neat summer clothes, married to a wild poet? Surely not.

His thoughts travelled back to Chaucer Road. Were things really going to change? His father was actually going to be interviewed for the new job. But meanwhile there was another mystery. His parents were going off to spend a few days in Wiltshire and Debbie was going to stay with friends.

Simon had no idea what their visit was all about. It seemed to be connected with a letter which had arrived at 52 Chaucer Road from a firm of solicitors in Malmesbury, and Simon only knew that because he had picked up the letter when it dropped on their doormat and had seen the flurry it caused. His father had immediately arranged to take a few days off work. From then on Simon caught snatches of conversation which stopped abruptly whenever he entered the room.

He did manage to discover that it concerned the winding up the estate of a distant relative by marriage. His father revealed that much though he was deliberately evasive on details. The elderly man who had died was on Mrs Pepper's side of the family but paradoxically his death did not seem to involve Jenny and Pop.

It was Simon who first caught sight of the ruined castle which stood on the hill overlooking the lush green valley in which Livensby, Jenny and Pop's home town, was situated. The sight of the familiar landmark never failed to produce a warm glow in Simon, associated with many happy holidays, the feeling of coming home.

This time his pleasure at returning was mingled with the eager expectation that here he might uncover a little more of the mystery he was trying to untangle. Here, in this part of the country, was the other half of his inheritance.

Simon was convinced that here, locked away in Jenny and Pop's old stone house with its Victorian furnishings and peaceful atmosphere, lay the answers to many of his questions.

His grandmother was happy to answer his questions. It took only a short time to dismiss some possibilities. Wedding pictures of Jenny and Pop established they had been married for forty nine years, and Simon knew his mother was not yet forty. That threw the "first marriage" theory out of the window.

Simon delightedly uncovered a dignified studio portrait of his great grandfather, the original owner of the magnificent fob watch. Not that there was any physical resemblance between the two of them. The picture showed a whiskered gentleman standing proudly alongside his delicate wife and their two little daughters.

"Nellie was just about four then," Jenny's voice was affectionate as she drew Simon's attention to her little sister in the picture.

"Did you ever have a brother Jenny?" Simon waited expectantly on her reply.

"No. That was a great disappointment to my father." Her reply gave rise to another idea.

"Would you have liked a son?" Simon was slightly embarrassed at the boldness of the inquiry.

Jenny showed no sign of being affronted. "Yes, I would." There was a pause. "I did have two boys but they both died within a few hours of being born. I was told I must not have any more children."

"You were lucky you had my mother." Simon was trying to digest this startling new piece of information. Jenny looked thoughtful. She nodded.

"They do say when one door closes, another opens." It seemed to Simon a strangely irrelevant comment.

One afternoon on impulse he set off for the parish churchyard, intent on finding his great grandparents' tomb. Pop's parents were buried sixteen kilometres away in the village of his childhood but he did not know if this was where Simon Jonathan had ended his days. It was a balmy English day with just a hint of a breeze, but even on a perfect afternoon like this the graveyard was forbidding. The overspreading arms of the ancient yew trees cast dark, gloomy shadows which even the most brilliant sun found hard to penetrate.

Simon had only a sketchy idea of the whereabouts of the grave. He had been brought here once by Jenny. Many of the stones had become cracked, covered with moss or barely legible, over the years.

He became absorbed in guessing some of the stories behind the simple hieroglyphics etched on the worn stones. There were Matthew and Clara who had both lived to a good age but who had lost eight of their eleven children in infancy. So much unhappiness. . .

Then there was Joshua who had succeeded in outliving three wives each younger than the one before! Simon pictured a small, mean man whose evil temper drove one wife after another to an early death.

A small much more modern stone tucked into

the line caught his eye. Elinor, only twenty-four when she died in a bombing raid in London. The name appealed to him. He visualized a beautiful young woman whose life had been tragically cut short.

There it was just nearby, the stone for which he was searching. Yates. That was the name of Jenny's parents. Ellen, the delicate young wife, had lain there for thirty years before being joined by her devoted husband, Simon Jonathan. It was a simple, dignified stone. Clearly someone had visited it very recently. It was neatly kept, and there were no sign of neglect or the weeds which disfigured so many of the surrounding graves. Someone had lovingly set out a vase of fresh flowers.

Simon wondered whether it was Jenny. She hadn't said anything but the flowers could not be more than two or three days old.

He leaned against the stone; a sense of family whelmed up inside him and he fingered the fob watch in his pocket with an aching pride. Aching perhaps because he knew he was asking for the impossible. He wanted so much to belong to Simon Jonathan, but the small nagging doubts about his parentage kept forcing themselves into his thoughts. And he knew too he wasn't prepared to give up the wayward red-haired poet he had built up in his imagination.

He wanted the best of both worlds – the solid respectability of these ancestors lying beneath his feet and what he hoped was the gifted brilliance of F.C.

He lay back. There was not another living person within sight or sound. The air vibrated with reassuring country noises. A tractor droned in the distance, birds chirped incessantly and an occasional car cut its way through the pleasant stillness.

Suddenly the peaceful air was shattered by an ambulance siren. Simon started homewards, thinking with pleasurable anticipation of the ritual of afternoon tea with his grandparents. First Jenny changed into one of her best dresses to show that the chores of the day were over. Then they would drink tea from thin china cups and eat slices of home-made fruit cake.

As Simon entered their road he noticed a little knot of women, their heads inclined towards one another. They looked up as he approached, several disappearing into their homes. He felt uneasy. One whom he recognized as his grandparents' next door neighbour, walked up towards him.

"Come into my house, Simon, I have a message for you."

Unthinkingly he followed her into the living room. A clock chimed. "What's happened?" he demanded breathlessly, fear striking suddenly.

"Sit down first," she said, kindly. "Your grandmother has been taken ill. They have taken her to hospital in the ambulance and your grandfather went with her. I said I would look after you until he came back."

"Is she going to be all right?"

"We don't know anything yet," said Mrs Davidson. "We'll have to ring up the hospital in about an hour. It will take the ambulance a little while to get to the hospital: it's quite a long way from here."

"But. . . what happened?" he blurted out.

"Your grandfather was too shaken to say much. Mrs Woodbyrne collapsed. She may have had a heart attack, but we don't know yet. The hospital have my telephone number if there is any urgent message."

"Can I go and see her?"

"Not yet I'm afraid. We'll just have to sit here and wait. I know how difficult it is," she added awkwardly, finding it hard to decide how best to handle the situation. She hardly knew Simon.

CHAPTER FIFTEEN

"My parents. They will have to know." Simon's efforts to steel his voice couldn't disguise the cracked, wobbly sound.

Mrs Davidson assured him she would ring as soon as the news was a little more positive. She bustled about making a cup of tea. Simon couldn't focus his attention.

Inwardly he was pleading that Jenny would be spared. He even tried pledging his own future good behaviour if this would ensure her recovery. He hardly heard Mrs Davidson's chatter. The old photographs he had been looking at so recently flashed in front of his eyes.

Everything took so long: ringing the hospital, contacting the Peppers. The hospital was cagey. Mrs Woodbyrne was in an oxygen tent. She had had a heart attack. But they allowed themselves to make slightly optimistic noises. Meantime Pop would be sleeping there until she was out of danger.

Simon's parents would travel up the next day and he was to spend the night with the Davidsons.

He went into the empty house next door to collect his nightwear and toothbrush. The grandfather clock, ticking away the minutes slowly and deliberately, resounded through the silent house. There was the tray laid out with an orange cake Jenny had made that morning. Mrs Davidson picked it up to take it home. It was sacrilege, thought Simon, that anyone should want to eat it now.

Without Jenny and Pop the house seemed dark and oppressive, even shabby.

Next morning the news from the hospital was more hopeful and there was plenty to do to prepare for the arrival of his parents. Simon was sent off with a shopping list, but though people were talking and jostling cheerfully along the busy shopping street Simon went about like a zombie. It seemed incredible to him that life went on, totally oblivious of the battle one old lady was fighting.

The Peppers had driven straight to the hospital. They were tense but hopeful when they returned to the house. Mrs Pepper set about preparing a meal. Finding things was no problem as each article seemed to be still in the familiar places she recalled from childhood.

Debbie clumsily knocked over a jug. It smashed on the floor. Her mother snapped, "Jenny had kept that for fifty years. You've been here an hour and it's broken. We have never had a year like this one," she commented wearily. "It has been one thing going wrong after another, ever since the start of the summer." Mr Pepper looked as if he wanted to disagree but changed his mind.

Simon realized sourly that his mother dated their

ill luck from the news that he had won the poetry prize. It was obvious too that his father's new job – it was now official – was dismissed as ill-fated. Mrs Pepper hated change.

Mr Pepper could stay in Livensby only a couple of days, but the rest of the family was to remain as long as they were needed.

Two things occupied all Mrs Pepper's thoughts and conversation: what would happen to Pop if Jenny did not recover, and the upheaval the new job would bring to life at Chaucer Road. Mr Pepper was unusually quiet and withdrawn on both topics.

All the old self-confidence seemed to have evaporated when he strolled down to the woods with Simon and Debbie the following morning. Lost in his own thoughts he seemed only to catch the tail-end of their remarks.

Debbie, who was unable to sustain gloom and anxiety for long, chased around trees escaping imaginary bears. Simon tried to find out about his father's new job but the replies came in half sentences.

When they reached the wide shallow river at the foot of the woods Mr Pepper settled himself down on the river bank while Simon and Debbie chased each other across the stepping stones. Wearying of the sport long before his sister, Simon clambered back to the bank where his father rested.

It was hot in the brilliant sunshine and Simon was startled to see his father shivering.

"What's wrong, Dad?"

"I'm just worried," answered his father. Simon was shocked to see how worn and vulnerable he looked, the harsh sunlight highlighting the deeply etched lines on his face.

"I just hope I'm doing the right thing."

"You mean about the job?"

His father nodded.

"It means a great deal of extra responsibility and a very heavy workload for the first year or two. I don't know if I should have taken it on. I will have to leave everything else to your mother to cope with and now there is all the extra worry about Jenny and Pop." Simon couldn't see the problem.

"Mum's healthy enough," he said.

His father shivered again and Simon wondered if his worrying was just a cover for his own lack of confidence.

"I was promoted once before a long time ago." The voice was flat and unexpressive. "But I had to give it up because your mother was ill. It was when you were very small and there was so much to do at home. It hurt to give it up then. Now I think that perhaps I'm too old for it."

Mr Pepper looked crumpled and dejected.

Simon tried to think of something encouraging to say but everything sounded stupid and hollow. Anyway his father was far too absorbed in his own thoughts to pay any attention. This was the first time he had ever glimpsed the uncertainty behind the bold front Mr Pepper presented to the world, and Simon suddenly felt very protective towards his father.

By the time they had returned to his grandparents' home Mr Pepper was more like his old self. That afternoon he was going home and Simon wished he could help his father grapple with his problem.

Jenny made slow but steady progress, and Pop came home to sleep. When he wasn't hospital visiting he sat around the house, his large frame looking sad and powerless. One day, assured that Jenny was now out of danger, he agreed not to go to the hospital. He was too weary. Simon could go in his place.

When they reached town Mrs Pepper remembered she had to call at the bank before it closed, and she left Simon at the hospital entrance, with directions to find the ward.

Simon felt a rising sense of panic as his mother vanished out of sight. He wished she had not gone. He had never seen anyone who was seriously ill before and he didn't know what to expect.

When he reached the ward it was to be confronted by a great deal of bustle with screens placed round Jenny's bed. The doctors had not finished their rounds. He was ordered aside kindly and told he would have to wait a few minutes.

A little later a helpful sister arrived on the scene, crackling with starch. "It should be all right now," she said reassuringly. "I'll just tell her you are here. Who shall I say it is?"

"I'm her grandson, Simon."

He was waiting outside the ward door. He heard her voice as she took away the screens. "It is your grandson, Mrs Woodbyrne, he has come to see you."

"I have no grandson." Jenny's voice was shaky but decisive. "Both my baby boys died."

"You are getting confused, my dear," answered the nurse soothingly, propping up her pillows. "It is Simon, your grandson. I have never seen such bright red hair."

"Oh Simon," Jenny answered weakly but rather irritably. "Why didn't you say so in the first place?"

CHAPTER SIXTEEN

Jenny was home, but still very weak and the Peppers were preparing to leave Livensby. Mrs Pepper had arranged for people to come in and help. The district nurse would call daily, the pantry was full and every room in the house had been turned out. "You won't need to cook for a few days," she told Pop.

"Will you go down to the shops and get me three bunches of flowers?" she asked Simon. "It will brighten up the rooms; they look so dark."

Simon spent a long time in the florist's. The flowers were so expensive. His mother had given him £3, which he thought was a surprisingly large sum, because she was always very careful with money. He chose a delicate bunch of freesias, pink, yellow, white and blue and two bunches of tall stately flowers, he wasn't sure what they were, one icy pink, the other a deep russety gold.

His mother was delighted with his choice. The gold flowers she put in the dining room with its deep brown furniture and curtains and the pink ones went in what was always known as the "blue room", the rarely used sitting room which had deep blue furnishing and a grey carpet.

His father arrived to pick them up that evening. Jenny looked tired but cheerful, and Simon thought she would be much happier when there were fewer people bustling around, constantly fussing.

Only a biting cold wind stopped the clouds from unloading their contents as the Peppers loaded up the car the following morning.

Debbie kept dancing about demanding attention just as they were humping out a case or struggling to tie things to the roof rack. "Please take her out for half an hour," Mrs Pepper appealed to Simon.

Simon was quite happy to escape from all the commotion. Besides he had a sudden urge to say goodbye to his great grandparents, Simon and Ellen, lying in the churchyard. Debbie accompanied him cheerfully.

"Isn't it lovely and spooky?" she said gaily, peering at the stones and trying to make sense of them. He pointed out the stone that marked where the Yates were laid to rest. "They were Jenny's parents," he explained. She stared fascinated.

Simon noticed that the weeds had begun to grow over the grave. But the flowers he had seen before had been removed. Someone had been tending another grave nearby. Elinor's. A little vase of fresh freesias stood by the stone. Pink, yellow, white and blue. They were the flowers he had bought for his mother just the day before.

CHAPTER SEVENTEEN

Simon and Morgan had set out the chessboard but they weren't really concentrating on the game. Morgan was eagerly digesting the latest developments in Simon's investigations.

Neither boy could decide how much credence to give to Jenny's announcement that she had no grandson. "Old people do ramble on," commented Morgan sagely. "Perhaps she was given a lot of drugs in hospital, and she thought she had gone back to her youth."

"Anyway we will soon know for sure," Morgan's manner was crisp and authoritative. "I swotted up that library book about tracing your ancestors during the holidays and we can. . . "

The front door bell rang. Simon went to answer the door. The boys had the house to themselves. The rest of the Pepper family had gone to a local fete.

A large station wagon was parked outside their house and Simon found himself confronted by an earnest young man who explained he had called to collect jumble for the Boys' Brigade.

Mrs Pepper said she would definitely have it ready for me," the caller said when Simon explained that his parents were out. "I have managed to borrow an estate car today to go round and collect it all!"

"Well, I can't really help. . . " began Simon.

"Couldn't you look?" The young man was pressing.

Simon had a hazy idea there was some jumble. He searched in the obvious places without success. Then he remembered how cross his mother had been when Debbie began reclaiming old toys from the pile. Of course, that was it! His father had put it in the attic.

"You'll have to come when my father's at home," he told the caller, explaining the dilemma.

But the young man was not to be dismissed so easily. Eventually Simon decided it was easier to give in than to argue. Unenthusiastically he agreed to fetch a step-ladder from the garage.

A small trapdoor above the upstairs landing opened into the dark, cavernous attic. The step-ladder wasn't really quite tall enough to make the ascent easy, so the young man helped to hoist Simon up. The large carton of jumble was balanced just near the trapdoor. The caller stood perched on top of the steps ready to take the box as Simon lowered it carefully.

"Can I give you a leg down?" Simon declined. He discovered a certain challenging mystery about the dark shapes which loomed around him. "Morgan! Fetch me the torch from the kitchen cupboard I want to have a look around."

The young man departed and Simon edged himself gingerly across the wooden joists. Morgan passed up the torch and Simon directed little pools of light around the black, draughty attic.

Here and there large, shapeless bundles emerged in the torchlight, huge spiders' webs hung from beam to beam and in the middle of it all stood the ominous bulk of the water tank. The atmosphere was cold and forbidding. Morgan's owlish eyes appeared over the rim of the opening, eager to join in the exploration.

Morgan was a thickset, heavy boy, and as Simon tugged on his arm he felt himself falling backwards. He hit a carton which fell on to its side.

Morgan was fumbling in the darkness. "For goodness sake mind you stay on the wooden bits or you'll fall through the plaster!"

Simon shone his torch on the carton which had spilled out its contents. There were baby's bootees, tiny pairs of shoes, a cot blanket, a little sunsuit, a baby's hair-brush. . . even rubber ducks he could remember playing with in the bath years ago. His mother had stored away all the mementoes of their early childhood. He put the carton back into position.

"Shine the torch in this direction," Morgan demanded. He had crawled along one beam into the depths of the attic. "There's an old briefcase here." Simon did as he directed.

"It has some initials on it," said Morgan. "P or F. I'm not sure which," he said slowly straining his eyes on to the dilapidated case. "Then either C, or G."

It was a few seconds before Simon recognized the significance of the letters. "Stay there," he ordered excitedly." He scrambled over to Morgan and directed the full beam of the torchlight onto the case. The initials might certainly be F.C. The leather was old and peeling and the outline of the gold letters blurred.

Simon began to fumble agitatedly at the clasp. It seemed to be locked.

"Come on. Let's take it down to the daylight," said Morgan sensibly.

Covered with dust and cobwebs, they clambered back to the aperture. Morgan held the briefcase while Simon lowered himself down, his legs dangling above the steps trying to gain a footing.

Morgan passed down the precious briefcase. Simon impatiently directed Morgan's legs onto the step-ladder before devoting his energy to unclasping the rusty, old lock. Clearly it had once been an expensive case. The leather was still soft and supple.

Simon fumbled clumsily with the lock but suddenly it gave way. Inside was a pile of rough papers, covered in the same flowing, distinctive handwriting though marred by innumerable crossings out and scribblings in the margin. It was the writing of an impatient person, someone who was never satisfied with what he had done.

Simon began to read one sheet. "In another land," he read aloud hesitatingly, "the lonely hoodlum stumbles to the night's last bright island and rests awhile in the cone of its silent security before he braces himself for the emptiness behind his front door the two existences which touched once briefly in another land."

As he read his voice found a rhythm and pattern. Only gradually did it dawn on him. It was a poem!

He searched hastily through the rest of the papers but there was no name, no signature. Just page upon page of writing, all revealing the same painstaking effort to find just the right word or phrase. Simon read one or two. Unhappy, disturbing and haunting. . .

He scanned the pages rapidly, searching for clues to the identity of the writer. But there were no letters or other documents. Just unfinished poems.

Simon was tingling with excitement. No question now about this man being a figment of his imagination. But who was he and where did he fit into the family?

"Let's go back to the attic. We might find something else." Morgan was now as excited as Simon.

Back up in the attic it was hard to make sense of the numerous boxes and cartons stored there. Old curtains, Christmas decorations, lamp shades, a broken record player that had long since been unable to produce a note. Did his parents ever throw anything out?

In their impatience they opened the same cartons again and again. It was hard to be systematic when they could only work in a small pool of light. Once or twice Morgan stumbled. Simon's heart missed a beat in case he slipped between the gaps in the wooden joists. It was not a pleasant place to be. Despite the bright sun outside there was a strange, cold, windy feeling in the attic, and the shadows beyond the range of the torchlight loomed large and menacingly.

"I have found something." There was a note of triumph in Morgan's voice. "Old photographs. They might tell us something."

"Let's take them downstairs." Simon was relieved of a chance to get back into the daylight.

Simon went first. Morgan passed him the bag and Simon steered his friend's legs back on to the stepladder before delving into its contents. He laid the pictures on the landing carpet.

Simon could make no sense of them. There was a very old photograph of a clergyman and what would appear to be his wife and child. A teenage boy playing cricket. An out-of-focus snapshot of a couple walking along a country path but. . . and here at last was a clue. . . Simon could just detect the outline of the Livensby castle in the background.

But it was Morgan who made the discovery. "Look." His voice was two octaves higher than usual. Simon glanced up sharply. A sudden shock passed through his whole body. The resemblance was undeniable. The face had the same bony structure, high cheekbones, deep set eyes and thin lips.

"We've found him," Morgan's voice had a crackly sound like an electric wire carrying a vital message. There was no doubt in either boy's mind. This was the F.C. Simon resembled. The poet himself.

Under the black and white picture was the name of the photographer. Leonard Able and an address in Leeds.

"Open up the frame," demanded Simon urgently. "There might be a name on the back of the picture."

Morgan slid the catches to remove the back of the frame. No message, just the words Christmas 1934. But the sloping writing was unmistakeable. This was the hand that had written the poems in the briefcase.

The boys eagerly sifted through the bag for a clue to his identity. There he was again pictured this time with a young fair-haired woman. Another snapshot showed him holding a baby. No more.

Livensby Castle in the background was the only evidence they had to work on.

The harsh sound of the telephone broke the boys' absorption. Simon went to answer, slightly drunk and dazed from the excitement of their discovery.

It was the high-pitched voice of one of his mother's talkative friends. "Your mother's on her way home, but she left her umbrella in the tea tent and I just wanted to let her know that I have got it safely. She doesn't need to worry about it and when she gets back home. . . " The voice went on and on.

"Thank you. I'll tell her," said Simon when he could get a word in edgeways. He realized they had to clear things away pretty quickly. He put the phone down as soon as he politely could and dashed upstairs.

"We've got to get the stuff back. They'll be home in a few minutes." He would confront his parents with the poems. But not just now. He needed time to think about it all.

Simon scrambled back to the loft and Morgan was just handing up the split bag when they heard the sound of the car in the drive.

The photo of F.C. lay on the landing. They had forgotten to put it back. "Take it home for me, under your jacket," Simon appealed to his friend. "There is just nowhere I can put it in my room. My mother is always going through my things."

In his own pocket lay a couple of pages of poems he had taken out of the briefcase.

CHAPTER EIGHTEEN

A strong draught whipped past Simon's ears as he and Morgan rode down the escalator past the pictures of bathing beauties adorned with moustaches, into the bowels of the mysterious, sunless world of the London underground.

Nobody cast a glance in their direction as the boys sat in the train, carefully counting each station. For them the expedition had all the sharp excitement of undercover espionage. They had done their homework, briefed themselves well and set out equipped with maps and timetables. Now at last the tube train was racing towards their goal.

They had succeeded in finding a highly plausible alibi. There was an international stamp exhibition at Olympia and the Peppers had agreed, after careful and consistent persuasion, to allow the boys to go alone to London as a special birthday treat for Simon.

The friends had certainly arranged to go to Olympia. There was no deception about that. But the most crucial visit came first. Their destination was Holborn, miles from Olympia, and they blinked as they emerged once more into the brilliant sunlight of the surface.

Maps before them, the boys made their way purposefully down Kingsway to number 10. So few of the large imposing shops and offices actually showed their numbers that they had twice walked past the house they wanted before they spotted the entrance tucked slightly away round a side turning. They went through the swing doors and found themselves in a long, open room more like a public library than anything else. It was crowded with people all reaching down from the shelves one volume, then another, and fighting for a space to spread them open on the desk tops.

It was Morgan who had painstakingly uncovered the fact that records of births, marriages and deaths were to be found in St Catherine's House, moved from their far more famous accommodation at Somerset House.

Here, tucked away in these huge volumes, were filed details of every family in the land and somewhere, if they could only uncover the right volumes, were the answers to the questions the two boys had been pursuing all summer. Now, for the first time, when the truth was so near at hand, Simon experienced a moment of apprehension. Did he really want to know it, come what may?

Morgan, held back by no such inhibitions, looked at the signposts. Marriage volumes bound in green were to the left, births in red to the right. He led the way towards the red shelves. It did not take long to discover they were organised chronologically with a separate volume for each quarter of the year.

There was no trouble about that – August 29, 1963. Most of the earnest visitors, armed with notebooks and pencils, were intent on much earlier records and the boys had this section to themselves.

"We need the volume for the third quarter of 1963." It was Simon who first located the relevant leather-bound book and lifted it carefully on to the desk top. He rested his hand on the binding, a sharp tingle of nervous expectancy racing through his body.

Inside the list of names was arranged alphabetically.

Simon turned the pages eagerly trying to find the Ps. Pa. Pe. – he was nearly there. Perry. Now he had overshot his target. Back successfully to Pepper. His finger followed the column down excitedly. Yes, there it was. Pepper, Simon Jonathan, August 29, 1963. With a code number. That was all.

He felt a crushing sense of anti-climax. "It doesn't tell you anything."

Morgan was better prepared. "You have to write down the number, then go to a counter and fill in a special form. Then you can buy a copy of the certificate."

The boys went to the back of the long room, filled in the necessary form, and waited in the queue to hand it over to a woman who sat behind a post-office type grille.

"That is two pounds, fifty," she said. "Can you collect the certificate tomorrow or do you want us to post it to you?"

"But we have come up specially. We want it now."

"No, I'm sorry." She left no room for argument. "You can see how busy we are. There is no way we can produce any copies straight away."

"Then it will have to be posted." Simon handed over the money and addressed an envelope to himself. The edge had gone off their expedition.

It had proved to be a costly exercise, but fortunately he had his birthday money with him.

Holding the receipt Simon glanced round the rows of shelves. All the details of his family were there somewhere on those shelves. F.C., too, must be recorded on some of those pages. His birth, perhaps his death as well.

He felt reluctant to leave. "Could we just look for my mother's birth certificate?" he asked hesitantly. Morgan's plans had not allowed for this, and he was getting hungry, but he reluctantly agreed.

"Well all right but we had better get a move on or we'll never get to Olympia. What year?"

"1935. April 1." There was a certain air of impatience about Morgan's back as he led the way along the shelves. It did not take long. Second quarter, 1935.

"There you are." No one was allowed to obstruct his way as he plonked the book on the wooden desk.

Woodbyrne was an unusual name, and Simon found it quickly. He ran down the list. No Christine. Not even a C. "She probably has another Christian name which comes first," suggested Morgan. But there wasn't even a C among the second names.

"Maybe it was 1934," suggested Simon sheepishly.

Morgan swapped over the books rather pompously, and put the other volume in front of his friend. No Woodbyrne here at all.

This time Morgan was prepared. 1936, second quarter he intoned. That brought no more luck. Neither did 1933 or 1937.

By now the boys had covered all the thirties unsuccessfully, and Simon was nonplussed. There was no question about his mother's birthday; the fact that it fell on April Fool's day had always been good for many family jokes. But the year? It must be in the early thirties. She had so often talked about childhood experiences during the war years.

"Come on, let's find your father instead," said Morgan.

That was easy. Simon knew the exact date, and only one Cyril Pepper had been born in Elbridge that particular year.

"Perhaps your mother is older than your father and so they keep quiet about it." Morgan spoke with the air of knowing about these things. "People seem to be embarrassed if the woman is older."

They went back another four years without success.

"Perhaps she has an official birthday, like the Queen, and keeps quiet about her real one," suggested Morgan after a fruitless search.

"She is not like that." Simon was defensive. Anyway he reasoned no one would *choose* April Fool's day. He paid for his father's birth certificate and arranged for it, too, to be posted to Chaucer Road.

He could not suppress a sense of triumph as they left the building. Two up, one down. That was progress at any rate.

Ahead lay the joys of lunch and then the stamp exhibition – Simon rated Morgan's idea for a birthday treat one of the best ever.

CHAPTER NINETEEN

Mrs Pepper ran to the front door. At first she did not recognize the tall figure of Mrs Thomas swathed in a full length black cloak with a scarf wrapped round her head and mouth to keep out the swirling fog. A couple of steps behind her stood the familiar, stocky figure of Morgan.

It was a wicked night. The thick, clammy fog had reduced the street lights to a tiny, flickering glow. "I didn't want Morgan to cycle here on his own," explained his mother.

A white and shaken Mrs Pepper led them into the front room. The warmth from the electric fire scarcely penetrated the chill atmosphere.

"Where can he have gone? And why?" Her voice was agitated. "I have telephoned everyone he knows. I just don't understand it." She was close to tears. "I was putting my ring away when I found the fob watch in my jewellery box. He was so attached to it. . . "

"I don't think," Morgan's voice was deliberate,

"he felt it really belonged to him."

Mrs Pepper looked puzzled. "Why on earth should he think that?"

"He got his birth certificate this morning," Morgan replied.

"Oh. That's what the letters were. But. . ." Mrs Pepper looked beseechingly at her husband. "But that doesn't explain where he is now."

"He wants to try to find his real mother."

"His what?"

"Look just sit down for a minute and we will try to sort this out." Mr Pepper pushed his wife gently into an armchair.

"I can't think why his birth certificate should cause so much bother," Mr Pepper mused. "Of course," he said without waiting for an answer as realization dawned on him, "it's the name."

His wife looked up quickly. "You were right," she said quietly. "We ought to have told him."

"Simon asked Morgan to look after this picture for him," Mrs Thomas produced the portrait of the bony-faced young poet from under the folds of her cloak.

"Oh!" Mrs Pepper shuddered. "I might have known that *he* would be behind this. We can't ever seem to bury him." Her voice was distraught. "What was Simon like when you saw him this morning?" she asked Morgan nervously. "I had to go out before he got up."

"He was furious," his friend replied. "He felt he had been tricked. The fob watch seemed to upset him more than anything. He felt he had no right to it."

"Look we have to find Simon as quickly as possible. Where could he have gone?" Mr Pepper appealed to Morgan.

"He said he was going to see Mr Marchington when he left our house this morning. He was going to give him a lot of poems he found in your attic and ask him to help to trace the poet. I thought he was just going round to his house – it's next door to the library – but when I passed it this afternoon I saw that it was up for sale and there is no one there."

"Where's he gone?" There was an urgency in Mr Pepper's tone.

"Perhaps he's gone to see if old Marchington is in his cottage. It's called Shelmer Cottage or something and I think it's near a place called Horsford."

"Simon couldn't cycle that far. It must be at least fifty kilometres. And he certainly wasn't dressed for this weather." Mrs Pepper's voice was shaky. "He has always had a bronchial chest just like my. . ."

"We'll have to find Mr Marchington's phone number." Mr Pepper obviously felt it was imperative to do something quickly.

"I know he's not on the telephone," said Morgan. "He doesn't approve of telephones, or cars, or television. He's always saying so." Morgan wouldn't forget that because they were the very things his parents objected to.

"I should check with directory inquiries anyway," said Mrs Thomas reasonably. "Just in case he has changed his mind. I'll go and make everyone a cup of tea." Mrs Pepper looked at her gratefully.

"We'll just have to drive down there," said Mr Pepper after he had confirmed that Morgan was right – there was no telephone subscriber called Marchington in the Horsford area.

"I think I would know where to find the cottage," volunteered Morgan. "He's described it to us so often."

"I don't suppose Simon will get that far," his father commented in what was intended to be an optimistic tone. "Certainly not in this weather. And Simon never did have much sense of direction."

"That's just the point," replied his wife weepily.

"I think I had better phone the police and let them know what is happening," said Mr Pepper.

"No! Oh, please God don't let Simon have an accident." Mrs Pepper walked over to where Mrs Thomas had laid down the photograph of the thin-featured poet. She picked up the portrait and stared at the face. "He is like a curse on this family," she said shaking the picture aggressively.

She laid it face down on the bookcase when Mrs Thomas gently handed her a cup of tea.

CHAPTER TWENTY

Mrs Pepper huddled in the back of the car peering out of the window for any sign of an accident. The police had had no reports of any cycling accidents. That was a relief.

The policewoman had been reassuring. "He'll be home soon I'm sure," she had said. "We get most of them back within twenty-four hours. The vast majority of youngsters don't seriously want to get lost. They are just trying to say something."

The words played over and over in Mrs Pepper's head. She looked guiltily at her husband's back humped over the steering wheel as he peered at the road ahead. Every now and then he wiped a hand across his forehead. It was a gesture he made whenever he was feeling tense.

Mr Pepper said little but his wife could read "I told you so" in the accusing angle of his shoulders and the particular edge to his voice.

His anxiety was tinged with a justifiable irritation that all this would never have happened if he had

had his way. For too long he had allowed his wife's feelings to overrule his own instincts.

Now, he thought grimly, it would have to change.

The car could do little more than crawl along. Morgan, who had told the Peppers such facts as the boys had uncovered, sat in the front seat with a map helping to navigate the route. He didn't ask any questions, and the Peppers were far too bound up in their own problems to offer explanations. Mrs Thomas had taken Debbie home with her when Morgan had offered to help the Peppers to find Shelmer Cottage.

Mr Marchington was their last hope. They had tried everywhere else, even phoning Livensby just in case Simon had got the train to Jenny and Pop's. The police had offered to send a local constable to Shelmer Cottage but Mrs Pepper was insistent that they should go themselves. Anything was better than sitting around the house, just waiting.

"I hope this doesn't make Jenny ill again." A new worry occurred to Mrs Pepper.

Mr Pepper groaned. Not because of his wife's remark but because they seemed to have taken a wrong turning. The fog was getting thicker and thicker. They shouldn't have set out. Mr Pepper was beginning to feel desperate. But it was too late now. They were committed. It would be as hard to go back as to continue.

Morgan was poring over the map with a torch. "I think we should be able to go through this way." He puzzled out the route. They were all shivering. The heater on the old car wasn't working, and the headlights weren't as strong as they might be.

Nobody said more than was strictly necessary.

Only regular stops to peer at road signs punctuated the dreary, frustrating journey. It seemed an eternity since they left Chaucer Road when Morgan commented, "I think the next junction should be Horsford. We should come across a pub called the Pemberton Arms, just before the turning we need." Morgan had a very clear picture in his mind's eye of the village pub as well as of the post-office-cum-shop from the wonderfully graphic descriptions Mr Marchington had given them. Nothing about the place or the people seemed to escape his all-seeing eye.

"I think we should call in at the pub and get some directions," said Mr Pepper. But on a night like this everything took longer than expected. First they overshot the pub and had to turn back. And just parking the car proved a slow operation. The pub was warm and inviting with a welcoming log fire, but the night was so grim that only one customer had braved the fog to seek its comforts.

"You look perished." The landlord was friendly.

"We are," replied Mr Pepper shortly. "We've got to get to Shelmer Cottage as quickly as possible."

"Expected there then?"

"Funny, someone else was looking for that." The other man looked up.

"A red-haired boy?" Mrs Pepper's voice was eager.

The man nodded. "He was in my shop not long before closing time. Couple of hours ago, I suppose. He asked the way to the cottage. Done in, he looked. And only wearing a thin jumper. I told him he would never find it with the fog coming in so thick. They've been putting out special warnings on the wireless. Anyhow he didn't say much and off he went. Don't know where. That's a difficult road down there at the best of times. It wanders right along the cliff edge."

"No!" The man looked at Mrs Pepper's drawn, pallid face.

"Goodness knows why people want to live in places like this," she shuddered gathering her coat closer about her.

"Well I don't suppose they was planning to entertain visitors in the. . . "

"If you can give us directions we must get going," interrupted Mr Pepper.

Back in the car again their progress was painfully slow. Mr Pepper kept having to wind down the car window to peer into the murky darkness to try to identify small landmarks as one turning after another led to different farms.

There were innumerable twists, bends and fork divisions. Suddenly the car jolted. Mrs Pepper shrieked as they were all thrown forward. There was a crash of grinding metal and the jarring sound of the brakes.

Mr Pepper leapt out of the car. Under one wheel lay Simon's bicycle. A tangled mess. He was down on his hands and knees shouting. "Simon. Simon." A groan came from nearby. Simon lay in a ditch. "It is my leg," he gasped. "I can't move it."

"How long have you been here?" Mrs Pepper wrapped her coat around Simon.

"Hours," he groaned painfully. "There must have been a stone in the road that threw me off my bike."

Mrs Pepper was crouching over Simon. "His leg," she said urgently to her husband, "you'll have to get a doctor. Something is wrong. It must be broken. Hurry – it is so cold here." She took off her coat and wrapped it comfortingly round Simon.

Mr Pepper lost no time in following her bidding. Morgan meantime was busy. He had taken a torch from his pocket and was peering carefully around the hedgerow. He gathered up the sodden sheets of poems which lay scattered around. He knew just how much these papers meant to Simon.

CHAPTER TWENTY-ONE

It had been a long, wearisome night. The slow crawl to the hospital in the ambulance, the anaesthetic, the broken leg encased in plaster, the telephone calls to say Simon was safe. . . No one had had much sleep.

Simon was shivery but otherwise seemed to have no more serious complications from his time in the ditch.

The air in the tiny living room of Shelmer Cottage was strained as Mr Marchington went off to make coffee. Every now and then a light illuminated the greyness that lay beyond the cottage windows. It was the rhythmic warning of the lighthouse beacon on the cliffs below.

No one seemed to want to speak. The only sound was the rolling of the thousands of tiny pebbles that tumbled on the beach below. Mr Marchington brought in a tray.

"I'm off to chop some logs."

"No," Simon and Mrs Pepper exclaimed simultaneously. "Don't go," the boy appealed.

"I don't want to interfere in family matters," the schoolmaster said.

Mr Pepper was decisive. Morgan and Mr Marchington should stay. They had both been drawn into the saga; they were part of the drama.

"If Simon starts by telling us what is bothering him," began Mr Pepper more hesitantly, "we'll try to explain whatever we can."

"I want to know who my real mother is," Simon sounded aggressive. "And why you have lied to me." He pulled the crumpled birth certificate out of his jeans' pocket.

In a second Mrs Pepper was kneeling at his feet, grasping his hands. "I am your mother, Simon. It's just the name that's different." Her son's expression was cold and unresponsive.

"Francesca Cressida Chalmers is the name I was born with – but I've never wanted anything to do with my father or his name."

"You mean that Jenny and Pop aren't your parents?" Mrs Pepper nodded. "Then it was all lies about the fob watch and being named after my great grandfather?" That really wounded, perhaps most of all.

"No. It isn't lies." It was Mr Pepper who spoke. "I think it is best if you start at the beginning," he said in a firm voice to his wife who sat staring at the fire, her face a frozen mask. "We agreed last night. . . "

"I wanted you to have a fresh start," Mrs Pepper grasped Simon's hands. "I didn't want you to have a millstone round your neck."

"Who do I look like? I want to know about F.C." Simon was impatient.

Mrs Pepper opened her bag and drew out the picture of the young man. "My father. Francis Chalmers."

"F.C." Simon's mind was turning somersaults." And he wrote poetry?"

"Yes – not that it was any good. But he wrote it all the time. We couldn't live on the occasional poems he had published in magazines. It was my mother who went out to work to keep us." There was undisguised bitterness in her voice.

"Well where is he now?"

"Dead. He died in the war when a bomb struck the house where we were living."

Simon's mind was racing ahead. "And your mother was called Elinor. You put flowers on her grave at Livensby."

Mrs Pepper looked taken back. "You've found out a lot. How did you know that?"

But Simon was too impatient to stop and explain. "But my grandparents, how do they fit into the picture? How can Simon Jonathan be my great grandfather?"

"Elinor was Jenny's younger sister," said his father. "But she was always know in the family as Nellie."

"She hated the name Nellie. Only my father used her proper name," said Mrs Pepper. "Anyway both my parents died in the bombing, and Jenny and Pop brought me up. They couldn't have children of their own so they pretended I was their own daughter." Mrs Pepper slotted the pieces of information in place.

His mother sipped her coffee silently. Nothing so far had dispelled the tension and strain which hung over the atmosphere in the room.

"Look we have had enough of half truths." There was a new edge to Mr Pepper's voice. "We have had far too much deception. So far it has caused nothing but pain and trouble. Simon could have died last night."

"It was my father's fault." Mrs Pepper's voice was remote. "He was like a curse on our family."

"Did he do something wrong?" Simon had to ask even though he wasn't at all sure he wanted to know.

"He killed my mother." The stark remark was greeted by a shocked silence. No one moved. For a few seconds the only sound was the crackling of logs in the fireplace.

"We were living in London in a ghastly tenement building. One night there was a terrible commotion. People were shouting and the house was full of thick, black smoke. I remember my mother dragging me out of bed, wrapping me in a blanket. She was shaking my father and yelling at him, 'The house is on fire!' She couldn't move him. He just grunted. She grabbed me and carried me downstairs. The passages were full of people shoving and elbowing one another in their panic to get out. We were coughing and choking. My mother put the blanket across my face.

"I'll never forget how marvellous the cold air felt when we got out of the building. My mother carried me across the road and set me down on the pavement. There was a great crowd of people watching the flames. She told me to stay put while she went back to look for my father."

"I could see her arguing with the firemen; they wouldn't let her go in. I saw her turn and walk away. She must have gone down an alleyway lower down the block so that she could slip in the back way. They found her body on the back stairs." There was a pause while Mrs Pepper fought to control her voice. "Everyone else in the house was saved, except my parents. My father never got out of bed. I stood on that pavement for hours."

Tears were rolling down Mrs Pepper's face.

"But," Simon remonstrated, "that doesn't mean he killed your mother. Perhaps he was ill."

"He was drunk." All the pent up hatred of years spilled out in her words. "All he thought about was himself and his work, never the fact that my mother was expecting a baby."

"There had been an awful row that night. He took my mother's wage packet from the mantelpiece and stormed out. She was weeping. I think he had probably had some work rejected because I remember him throwing a pile of papers on the fire."

Simon listened. But even the full horror of the story could not diminish the bond he felt with F.C. He could understand why he wouldn't get out of bed that night and the paralysing pain of misery and rejection. He had felt the same as he lay in the ditch last night.

"But your name?" It was Morgan, sitting owl-like listening to the narrative, who asked.

"I wanted nothing to do with my father, just to blot him out of my existence. My name reminded me of him. I was named Francesca after him, and Jenny told me that my father chose Cressida because both the world's greatest poets had written about her. I hated both names. Luckily my parents had nicknamed me Chrissie so when I went to live with Jenny and Pop all my friends assumed that my real name was Christine. I was quite happy; it was so nice and ordinary. I wanted to belong to Jenny and Pop. They were so good to me. That was why I called myself Woodbyrne. They weren't happy about it at all, and they would never let me call them mother and dad."

"That explains of course, why there was no Christine Woodbyrne in the register of births," mumbled Morgan.

"And that I can't inherit Pop's dia – whatnot."

Mrs Pepper hardly noticed their interruption. "Jenny and Pop kept trying to tell me my father had been a brilliant man."

"I think he was," Mr Marchington interposed quietly. "I was reading the poems last night and some of them are really very fine."

"Jenny and Pop didn't stand on the pavement that night watching the flames," said Mrs Pepper slowly. "They had no idea what our lives were like. My mother used to creep around so as not to disturb my father. We were terrified of his moods. She used to take me out for long walks so he could get on with his writing. The rooms were always cold and damp because we never had enough money for heating. *And* he always had to have the seat nearest the fire and the biggest helping of food."

"How did your mother meet him?" Simon asked.

"He came to teach at the local grammar school, straight from Oxford. He couldn't go to the war because of his bad chest. Jenny told me that he had such radical ideas that my grandfather wouldn't have him in the house. He used to talk to the pupils about them. The headmaster and the governors didn't like it and eventually they asked him to leave the school after he told one class that he didn't believe in God. That was very shocking in those days. Anyway he didn't care. All he wanted to do was to write.

He probably thought it was going to be so easy. The first poem he ever sent to a magazine was published. Jenny told me it was in *The Listener*. But when my parents ran off to London, he had one rejection after another. Every now and then one would be published – and my mother would be so pleased she would sit staring at the magazine page and my father's name."

Simon's thought turned to 52 Chaucer Road and the Peppers' quiet, ordered life. It all began to make sense to him now. His mother was trying to recreate the calm, unruffled world that belonged to Jenny and Pop. Marrying his own father she couldn't have chosen anyone more different from F.C. She wanted a life utterly removed from the painful chaos of her early years.

"Yes, but the baby photos," puzzled Morgan when there was a lull in the narrative. "Why were there no pictures of Simon?"

Mrs Pepper looked alarmed and cast her eyes up to her husband imploringly.

"You mother was very ill after you were – "

"I don't want to talk about that," said Mrs Pepper quickly. "There is no need to go into that."

"I think there is." Simon was surprised at his father's firmness. For years he had refused to upset his wife. But just lately, perhaps because of his new job, Mr Pepper seemed to have developed a much greater confidence in his own judgement.

"We are not sweeping anything else under the

carpet. I am sure Simon will understand." He looked at his son. "After years of trying to pretend that her father had never existed you can imagine what a terrible shock it was to your mother when you were born looking so like him. Even in your baby features there was absolutely no doubt about the resemblance. It was months before your mother could cope on her own. It was more than just being upset – it was an illness. That was when I had just had my first promotion, but I had to give it up because there was so much to do at home. My mother used to come to our house every day. It was a long time before your mother was convinced that though you might look very like her father, you would be quite a different. . ."

Now Simon could understand his mother's white and shaken face when he had told her about the poetry prize. His mother's thoughts too had turned to that day.

"When you stormed out of the house on the day you won the poetry prize it could have been my father all over again," she said interrupting her husband's narrative.

"You can hardly blame Simon for that. He has been made the scapegoat for everything that has gone wrong this year." Mrs Pepper looked at her husband with a startled expression: he so rarely raised his voice.

Mr Marchington kneeled down to poke the fire. He tried to change the subject. "I don't think there is any doubt that F.C. was gifted," he commented placatingly. "Or that Simon is too."

Mr Pepper looked interested. "We have box upon box of his poems at home. Strangely enough it is only a few weeks since F.C.'s father died. My wife never had anything to do with him, but in his will he said he wanted Chrissie to have all her father's possessions that were left. We collected cases of them. My wife didn't want to look at them so we put them all away in the attic."

"Do you know I would love to look at the poems and have a shot at editing them." Mr Marchington's face lit up with enthusiasm. "Perhaps I could see them?"

"No," said Mrs Pepper sharply. "Surely now at last we can bury him and forget about him. He has spelt disaster to everyone and everything he came into contact with. I am sure it would bring more bad luck. . . "

Mr Pepper looked at her thoughtfully. He hesitated. He hated to see his wife upset. Perhaps she was right. Perhaps this was the time to bury the past. He nodded slightly.

"I would have thought," said Mr Marchington thoughtfully, "that your mother would have liked the poems to be published. She obviously believed in them and if they were saved, it would make the tragedy a little less pointless."

Mrs Pepper looked as though she might be persuaded by the schoolmaster's words. Her husband was convinced. He issued an invitation to Mr Marchington to visit them at Chaucer Road. "We'll get everything down from the attic," he promised.

CHAPTER TWENTY-TWO

Mr Pepper was as good as his word. An invitation was dispatched to Mr Marchington within days of the family's return home.

The boxes were brought down from the attic. Simon with his leg encased in plaster could not help, so Morgan was invited round to give a hand in lifting them down and to be present at the general opening up.

There were other reasons too. Mr Pepper was urging that they should leave Chaucer Road. It wasn't just that he was spending two hours a day in his car travelling to work; he wanted a move to mark a dividing line in the life of the family.

Simon's mother read the house prospectuses. She didn't openly oppose the idea but she always found something wrong. She clung firmly to what was familiar.

"Now we've ironed out everything we're all right here," she suggested. But the ironing out Simon noticed had not brought his mother any new lightness of heart. Anxiety and strain still hung around her.

She was even quieter than usual. The photo of F.C. had disappeared, and the subject of her father, along with all the disclosures at Mr Marchington's cottage, had become a closed book once again. Simon's mother became increasingly edgy as the date for Mr Marchington's visit approached.

Simon knew his father was worried about her. His mother wasn't sleeping well and though she produced the usual family meals, she didn't eat much herself.

Simon felt that his father was much happier in himself. He had a new buoyancy and optimism as he hummed snatches of popular songs to himself. It was a long time since Simon had heard his father singing. And there was a new lightness in his step.

The new job had not presented any problems. Mr Pepper worked long hours, but everything was well within his capabilities and he seemed much more self assured. Simon noticed that his father did not seem to care *quite* so keenly for all the routines at Chaucer Road and sometimes the lawn was not cut twice a week, and the dead heads not instantly removed from the roses.

Mrs Pepper's anxiety still cast a shadow over the household. Simon didn't believe they would ever move – even though his father was tossing out of the attic the inevitable rubbish of years of family life.

Morgan's help in retrieving two large boxes and a leather suitcase embossed with the initials F.C. from the attic was more well-intentioned than practical. But now the cases stood in the hall awaiting the arrival of the schoolmaster. The opening was to have something of the ceremony of Christmas. Everyone was to be present and there was to be no peeping until the appointed hour.

Simon felt a mounting sense of anticipation as the time drew near. It had all the excitement of treasure trove.

"Not Pandora's box I hope," was the wry comment of his less enthusiastic mother.

When the actual moment came there was a complete lack of system as people set about diving into the boxes. Simon had to rely on the others handing him bundles of papers to examine. Debbie raced around adding to the general confusion, and excited voices were raised as someone held up a new discovery from the depths of a box.

Initialled cuff links, old school ties, certificates. . .

Even Mrs Pepper, hovering on the sidelines, began to be drawn in. "They even kept his glasses and shaving mirror," she said in a voice of quiet surprise as she retrieved the articles from the floor. Simon was reading through a pile of old school reports. He smiled; they had such a familiar ring. Francis had excelled at English but little else.

"Look," Morgan took some papers over to Mrs Pepper. "It is a children's story. 'The Magic Marble'," she read aloud. "I had forgotten all about those stories." The hostility had melted from her voice. She knelt on the floor, oblivious of everyone else, re-reading the tales her father had created for her as a little girl.

Meanwhile Mr Marchington was putting scores of poems into piles, stopping to read one occasionally. He took one over to Mrs Pepper. "I don't think you can doubt that he loved his wife and daughter," he said quietly. "It is all here." He handed her a sheet.

Mrs Pepper took the poem and looked wonderingly at the schoolmaster's face.

"He wasn't any better at games than Simon," Morgan laughed as he read a report. "Francis lacks team spirit. Poor coordination."

"Francis needs to respond more positively to helpful criticism," he read aloud enjoying the joke.

Mr Marchington was busy at his self-appointed task. "I'll have a marvellous time working through these. You'll have to give me a hand, Simon." The boy was delighted.

Mr Pepper wasn't looking at the papers. His attention was caught by his wife's expression. Her features had relaxed as she returned to reading her childhood stories. She smiled slightly. It was only Debbie's excited shriek that brought her back to the present.

"Look. I've found a gold ring."

Mrs Pepper struggled on to her feet, her legs cramped with crouching on the floor, and hurried over to her daughter who had slipped the man's ring on her finger.

"Just let me show you something," she said, gently removing the ring from the girl's finger. She carefully felt round the ring. "It is a special keepsake and it should open up." Her fingers fumbled with the fastening for a minute or two as the others gathered round fascinated.

Suddenly it sprang open. Inside were two locks of hair. One bright red, the other deep brown.

She lifted the red hair out of the ring and placed it against Simon's. The colour was identical. "My father's hair," she explained. "The other is my mother's."

She put the hair back in the ring and closed it down. "It was my father's ring. Here Simon, try it on." He held out his hand and his mother put the ring on one of his fingers. He looked up at her face.

She was smiling as she hugged him.

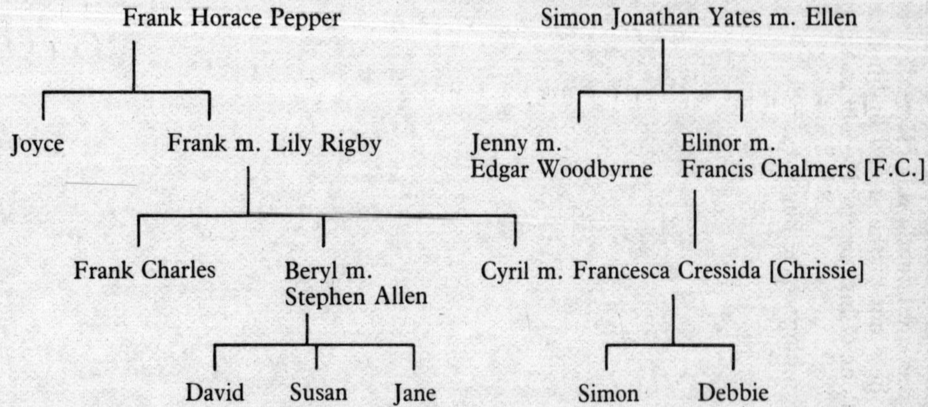

Simon's Family Tree

OTHER HIPPO BOOKS
FOR YOU TO ENJOY

THE "FAMOUS BATTLES" SERIES

by Roger Gates

These three history/activity books bring some of Britain's major air, land and sea battles to life. They are packed with facts about the everyday lives of the men involved – their training, uniforms, and even what they ate – as well as detailed vivid accounts of all the decisive battles.

Each book includes activities such as a board game to make and play, and there are dozens of full-colour stamps to stick in as you go through each book.

The English Civil War 0 590 70008 1 90p
The Battle of Britain 0 590 70007 3 95p
The Battle of Trafalgar 0 590 70027 8 £1.25

SEA CHANGE

by Anne Knowles

Megan Garreg is left in charge of a sheep farm at the busiest time of year, and her favourite escape is to the cliffs where she can gaze into the water – and at Abergwent, the drowned village that lies in its depths.

She is glad when Owen Morgan, a stranger she meets on the beach, agrees to help her on the farm, and together they cope with the lambing and with sheep rustlers. Owen gradually tells Megan about his past, which is strangely linked with the drowned village, but neither of them realises that history may be about to repeat itself...

ISBN 0 590 70024 3

65p

HENNY TAKES A HAND

by Barbara Paterson

Life is never dull when Henny is around! She's resourceful, inquisitive and enterprising, and never at a loss for an idea – though some of her schemes have unexpected results.

Whether she's outwitting the school bully, trying out free samples from the icecream shop, helping a neighbour to move house or trying to win a family hoiday competition, funny things always seem to happen when Henny takes a hand.

ISBN 0 590 70009 X

95p